LOVE
WITHOUT
SHAME

Dave Wyrtzen

25 25thChapter

Love Without Shame

Copyright © 2013 by David B. Wyrtzen
Edited by: Jenae Edwards

Re-Published by 25th Chapter
      313 Woodridge Drive
      Tuscaloosa, AL 35406

Cover design: Harvey Edwards

First printing 1991 by Discovery House Publishers is affiliated with RBC Ministries, Grand Rapids, Michigan 49512.

Printed in the United States of America

Library of Congress Cataloging-in-Publication Data
Wyrtzen, David B., 1949—
Love Without Shame / by David B. Wyrtzen. p. cm.
ISBN 978-0-9838645-2-3

1. Sex—Biblical teaching.
2. Sex—Religious aspects—Christianity.

To Mary,
my wife

Contents

Introduction

In our culture no one needs to be told that S-E-X is powerful and pervasive. Advertisers spend billions associating their products with "sexiness"; movies and novels juice their sales by including steamy "love" scenes; and if we're honest, we will admit that sex is on our minds more often than not. Because this drive is so powerful, our desire for sex can be an explosive problem. Guilt, teen pregnancy, STDs, adultery, abortion, pornography, incest, and rape unveil the battle-scarred terrain resulting from our misuse of sex.

To meet these threats, we struggle to develop a strategy for defense. Parents, teachers, and clergy compete over who is responsible for teaching the "facts of life" to the next generation. And in the midst of our bickering, we cast the blame on others while our culture and the media continue to teach our children and us a distorted view of sex whether we like it or not.

Recently I asked some students to tell me how they learned about sexual intercourse. Their responses illustrate the pain that can comes from false information and the need for mature, moral adults to unashamedly tell the truth about sex to the younger generation.

"My dad had *Playboy* books and other pornographic material in our house. One day when I was a sixth grader I stumbled upon them and—the eyes take a picture. It's been a battle ever since."

"I came to know about sexuality three ways: by experimenting at the age of seven, through pornographic literature and movies, and by talking with my friends."

"I learned about sex the hardest way anyone can learn. My ex-boyfriend, a supposedly strong, active Christian, raped me."

"My mom was always very honest about sexuality. She sat down with us, beginning about age seven, and explained a lot. Slowly through the years she shared more and more. She always encouraged us to ask questions and be honest with her."

9

"How did I learn about sexuality? As a little girl in the second grade through an incestuous relationship with my older brother."

"I learned about sexual intercourse when my parents gave me a book to read from a prominent Christian leader."

"How did I learn about sexuality? I didn't know anything about it for the longest time. My parents are very loving. Dad's a preacher. They always showed their love and care towards me. I could have asked my parents about sex, but I really never thought about it. My dad did hand me a book about it, but it was boring. I didn't think I needed to worry about it until I got married. Then my first *real* boyfriend came around. He was older than me. I was this little, innocent girl who attracted this experienced, popular, all-around great, nice looking guy. I thought he was everything. I practically worshiped him. You could almost call him my god.

When the subject of sex came up I told him that I was against having it before marriage. I was naive about what goes through a guy's mind when he thinks about women. One night, before I could say anything, he forced me to have sex. He was a guard on the football team, and I'm 5' 1" and weigh 106 pounds. In the midst of my tears I remember telling him to stop. At the age of fifteen my virginity was lost. I felt I had ruined my life forever, so to try to make things okay, I stayed with my boyfriend. During this time my values went down the drain. To make a long story short I got pregnant when I was sixteen. I … had an abortion, which goes against all of my principles. That is how I learned about sexuality! You could say I learned the hard way."

Do teenagers have to learn about sex the hard way? This cross section of responses reveals that children are learning fact and fiction about sexual relationships from peers, the media, relatives, and professionals. Naiveté does not protect them. Ignorance often leaves our children vulnerable to immorality's vicious abuse. The school of hard knocks can be cruel and leave ugly scars. As a father, educator, and pastor, I believe we owe it to the next generation to face our own sexuality and decide the truth about it. We must stop turning red and remaining silent. But if we are going to responsibly educate others about sex, we must first know the truth about sex ourselves.

Why not start with the One who created sex in the beginning? Only He can provide the truth about its purpose and its exhilarating pleasure. Only by remembering His original design, acknowledging the present perversion of His purpose, and listening to His solution can we use this "nitroglycerin within" to soothe our lonely hearts instead of blowing one another to pieces.

This is a book about the theology, not the biology, of sex. It explores what God's Word reveals about one of His most precious gifts to us. God does not blush when we ask Him about sex. As the Creator of this ecstasy, He desires adult believers to come to grips with their own sexuality from His perspective so that they can teach the truth about sexuality to the next generation. Why did He make a male and female to fit together? Was it only a practical solution to the need for population? Why has sex, intended to be a blessing, become such a problem for us? How can God's children recapture the sacred meaning of sexuality, and, make love without shame? Let's begin by going back to a time when sex and shame were not companions.

Part One

The Original Design

The man and his wife were both naked, and they felt no shame.

Genesis 2:25

Chapter 1

The Priceless Reflection

The bride's mother dabbed her eyes with a crumpled Kleenex. The bride's father stood resolutely between his youngest daughter and her husband-to-be. The audience fidgeted while the organist continued his processional at full stop, oblivious to the fact that the bride had already made her entrance and now clung nervously to her dad in front of the minister. Since flowers obscured his vision of the main aisle, the organist could not be blamed for continuing his push toward his grand finale. At last he found the harmonious concluding chord and the audience sat down to relax to the familiar introductions of the wedding ceremony.

Richard, the young seminary graduate—relieved that he had remembered to ask the audience to sit—cleared his throat and began his first wedding ceremony. This was not the same as sitting in a theology class, but the security of the printed page, stuck in the pages of his open Bible, steadied his quivering voice.

"On behalf of Gerald and Patricia, I want to welcome each of you to this joyous occasion as these two express their covenant vows to join together for life. There was a time when a man and woman's 'I do' could be depended upon for lifelong security, but it seems this day has largely passed. The fragile nature of the contemporary marital bond underscores the need for God's children to reaffirm the sacredness and endurance of the marriage promises. Marriage is not the creation of humankind but of the Creator, and Genesis takes us to the beginning, back to the first wedding ceremony."

To emphasize the imperatives of Scripture, Richard turned to Genesis 2 in his large black leather Bible. Few in the audience noticed. Most of the women were mentally debating the bride's choice of color for the bridesmaids' dresses. The majority of the men contemplated whether the reception would serve more than wedding cake and ginger ale punch. Richard's reading provided background noise for these more immediate concerns:

> *So the Lord God caused the man to fall into a deep sleep; and while he was sleeping, he took one of the man's ribs and closed up the place with flesh. Then the Lord God made a woman from the rib he had taken out of the man, and he brought her to the man.*
> *The man said, "This is now bone of my bones and flesh of my flesh; she shall be called 'woman,' for she was taken out of man." For this reason a man will leave his father and mother and be united to his wife, and they will become one flesh.* (Gen. 2:21-25)

The audience expected the usual period after "flesh," but Richard, absorbed in the text, continued to proclaim the next verse, "The man and his wife were both naked, and they felt no shame."

When Richard said the word "naked" connected to a man and a woman in a church, he stunned his daydreaming audience to rapt attention. The groom's red ears, the bride's flushed cheeks, and some stifled giggles from the audience indicated that Adam and Eve may have felt "no shame," but this group blushed plenty.

This young minister will learn that the traditional ceremony omits Genesis 2:25, and, thus, he will save himself and his audience some embarrassing moments in his next wedding. But the first wedding officiator did not blush, and He concluded His oration with this statement about sexual nakedness. Why did the Creator mention a husband and wife's nakedness at the first wedding? What was so different back in Genesis 1 and 2? Why was there no shame?

Back to the Garden

God's Goodness and the First Couple's Nakedness

I love doing premarital counseling. What better to give a young couple than an overview of God's blueprint for marriage as a wedding present? I always start with the foundation of marriage in Genesis 1

16

and 2 by asking the engaged couple this question: "Suppose someone came to you before you were married and gave you the keys to a million dollar home in Hawaii, featuring a Japanese garden overlooking the Pacific, and told you to enjoy it for a lifetime. He informed you that the refrigerator was stocked with all the food you could eat and all the beverages you could possibly drink; the bedroom was furnished with an immaculate king-size bed, and the bathroom boasted a Jacuzzi large enough to pass for a swimming pool. He then handed you a checkbook and said, 'Your account is inexhaustible. I want you both to enjoy one another and the beauty of your new home.' What would you conclude about the character of this benefactor?" Almost every couple I counsel responds to my question with, "What's the catch?"

Their cynicism exposes the doubting, distrustful Adam in all of us. Since the Fall in Genesis 3, our wariness concerning promises "too good to be true" is a protection against all kinds of con-artists seeking to deceive us. But God's goodness is not false. In Genesis 1 and 2, He had no hidden agenda.

God placed Adam in a perfect environment, told him to enjoy all the good fruit in the Garden except for one tree, and brought to him the most beautiful woman a man could imagine. He stood her before him naked and said, "Enjoy! This is your new ally." A man would be insane to put this data together and conclude that God his Creator was a scrooge, yet doubt concerning God's basic goodness and generosity started humankind's fall into sin. We must counter this stupid conclusion by learning and teaching our children to trust God's character—to believe that He is good. And His goodness includes His design for sex.

Satan wants us to believe that God hates the thrill of sexual union, that only by walking away from Him can we find pleasure and happiness, and that giving into our impulses gives us true freedom. But Genesis 1 and 2 counters this lie by telling the truth about the Creator. He not only gave Adam and Eve the most beautiful home ever built, but His first command was for them to make love and fill the earth with their children (Gen. 1:28). He was not only unashamed of their nakedness but invited them to enjoy one another's bodies (Gen. 2:24-25; Prov. 5:18-19). God created the passion and pleasure of sexual union.

Unashamed of Our Bodies

Down through the centuries, asceticism—the belief that sinful desires can be controlled and God can be pleased by the rejection of the physical body—has seduced the Christian church. This denial of the body led to our conclusion that the passion and exhilaration of intercourse, even in marriage, was sinful. Sex became a demon to be destroyed. This religious denial of God's good gift of the human body, including sexuality, represents one of Satan's most cunning deceptions, and a residual uneasiness concerning the physical body continues to plague some religious instruction about sex. Biblical marriages need to resist this lie and revel in the goodness and pleasure of physical union between husband and wife. God is Spirit as John 4:24 teaches us, but this emphasis on our immaterial nature should not cause us to negate our bodies. The Old Testament balances this union of both spirit and body by daring to present God in bodily form as He talks with Abraham (Gen. 18), and at Christmas millions celebrate the incarnation where the second person of the Trinity came to earth and revealed God to us in human form (Heb. 10:5; John 1:14). The resurrection gloriously transformed Jesus' earthly body into an eternal heavenly body, and when He returns He promises to work this same transformation in us (Phil. 3:21). This "bodily foreverness" warns against viewing our present physical body as simply a container for the important ingredients inside. The body is not the prison house of the soul. Our material and immaterial natures are united. Therefore we must not demean or be ashamed of the physical body God molded for us in the womb (Ps. 139:15).

While religious ascetics reject the human body, the secular Darwinist proclaims that humankind is only body. Materialistic evolutionists view human beings as merely sophisticated primates with the gift of speech. From this materialistic perspective human sexuality becomes a subcategory under the study of animal reproduction, and anthropologists argue over whether or not human sexual behavior developed out of the habits of gibbons or chimpanzees (cf. Tannahill, 18-22).

Though a trip to the monkey cage at any zoo will verify that God did use some similar external design patterns for human beings and apes, Genesis reveals that there is a chasm that forever separates us from them. This difference places the human act of making love in a completely different category than monkey mating. We must not malign the human body, but we must also remember that we are far more than just flesh and blood.

Back to Our True Value
No Shame in Reflecting Our Creator

> God said, "Let us make man in our image, in our likeness, and let them rule over the fish of the sea and the birds of the air, over the livestock, over all the earth, and over all the creatures that move along the ground."
> So God created man in his own image, in the image of God he created him; male and female he created them.
> (Gen. 1:26-27)

We find our true value not by looking around at the animal kingdom but by looking up to our Creator. Through the centuries human beings have insisted on kneeling before gods of gold and silver, whether they were the metallic figurines of the ancient world or the aluminum and plastic automobiles of the modern world. People bow down, worship, and pretend that this stuff gives life and importance. Throughout the Old Testament God ordered His people to have "no other gods before" Him (Ex. 20:3). But Genesis 1 tells us that God did make an image of Himself on earth—*us!*

Our worth is not calculated by the clothes we wear, the job we have, or the stuff we collect. God says we are priceless, not because of what we possess, but because of who we are. We reflect the ultimate King, the creator and sustainer of the universe. We are not ourselves gods, as some Eastern gurus would have us believe; we are the reflection of the

19

one true God. Anyone made like this supreme King need never feel inferior. So what does it mean that we are made in God's image?

Theologians continue to debate this mystery, but this should not keep us from building on some facts that are known about our inestimable price tag—"Made in the *imago Dei* (image of God)." The elusive internal qualities that make us like God give human beings a value that far exceeds that of animals.

To discover these distinctions let's begin by answering the question, "What is God like?" Only after we understand who God is can we discover which of His characteristics are evidenced in humankind. The first chapters of Genesis respond to these questions with two characteristics that God and humankind share: personality and companionship.

The Priceless Personality

Vintage blockbuster movies such as the *Star Wars* Saga have made Eastern religious ideas about "god" as an impersonal force part of pop culture. The academic study of theology in the West often turns God into the "ultimate rational mind." Neither "the force" of the East nor the "computer" of the West presents the authentic image of God. We need to rediscover the true God revealed in Scripture as a loving and just Father—a personal being who can not only think but who also feels and decides.

In Genesis 1 and 2, God speaks, works, plans, and enjoys. He introduces Himself not only as an engineer who rationally executes a skillful design plan, but also as an artist and poet who relishes beauty and enjoys companionship (Gen. 1:26; 3:8). He thinks. He feels. He is real.

And He reveals Himself as the disappointed creator: *"The Lord was grieved that he had made man on the earth, and his heart was filled with pain"* (Gen. 6:6); as the devastated lover, *"Rebuke your mother, rebuke her, for she is not my wife, and I am not her husband"* (Hos. 2:2); as the wooing suitor, *"Therefore I am now going to allure her; I will lead her into the desert and speak tenderly to her"* (Hos. 2:14); and as the restoring father, *"When Israel was a child, I loved him, and out of Egypt*

20

I called my son. . . . How can I give you up, Ephraim¹? How can I hand you over, Israel?" (Hos. 11:1, 8a).

At the culmination of the creative process this personal God sculptured Adam from the dust and fashioned Eve from his side. Adam and Eve were more than animated clay puppets. They, like their Creator, were personal beings who could reason, feel, and decide. Thus, they could enjoy companionship with one another and with their God. He gives us this gift of personality to each of us—the basis of human dignity, a gift with value surpassing time.

The denial of this divine gift is the breeding ground for sexual sin. Sex divorced from personalness mocks the image of God in man and woman. It becomes isolated as solely a physical drive, an animal instinct. Thus, our culture's denial of the human personality's distinctiveness as the reflection of the divine personalness is a major factor in the brutalizing of sexuality. Human beings who are taught that they are only highly developed brutes often behave like brutes. Rape, incest, and sexual abuse mean nothing when applied to apes or dogs. Animals do not think about ethics or have feelings about relationships, but human beings created in the image of God must.

We need to reaffirm our distinctiveness from the animal kingdom. Our homes must honor our children's growing ability to reason, to express emotions, and to make responsible decisions. We must refuse to value material things more than the people around us. Parents and children together must cherish the divine image in human life. This provides a powerful preventative inoculation against the abuse of the sex drive.

Homes that forget this pricelessness of personality fuel illicit desires in their children. During adolescence children will try to find a false, idolatrous identity in the intense sensations of their sex organs. These physical experiences divorced from personal closeness and devotion can provide electrifying pleasure, but they are as foolish as a toddler plugging a metal fork into a wall socket. Sex without intimacy yields burned out adults. Even segments of the secular world are beginning to preach the destructiveness of sexual involvement without personal intimacy (Shalit, *A Return to Modesty*).

21

The image of God informs us that we are personal beings distinct from animals; but it also tells us that we were built for companionship. Our Lord desires to be with us in our lives. He rejoices in the close friendships and relationships we enjoy with one another and with Him. The husband-wife relationship, above all other human relationships, proclaims the richest expression of this intimate companionship. So our children's sex education should begin with a dad and mom who value their distinct personalities and who cherish intimacy—the intimacy they enjoy with God and with one another.

The Perfect Companionship

> God said, "Let us make man in our image,". . . in the image of God he created him; male and female he created them....
> The Lord God said, 'It is not good for the man to be alone. I will make a helper suitable for him.
> (Gen. 1:26-27; 2:18)

Intimate companionship is so priceless and eternal it is part of the essence of God Himself. Within the unity of the one true God there is the eternal relationship of the Father, Son, and Holy Spirit. Matthew 28:19 explicitly states this oneness and equality of the three persons of the Trinity, while the creative group consultation in Genesis 1:26 implicitly illustrates the mutual involvement of the Father, Son, and Holy Spirit in the creation of man and woman. They think together, feel together, and decide together. The Trinity reveals an eternal companionship. Human beings, created as male and female, mirror this companionship, not in their sexuality, but in the desire for two distinct persons, a man and woman, to think, feel, and decide together in the marriage relationship. The companionship of the Trinity gives significance to companionship in marriage.

Ten times in Genesis 1 and 2, God pronounced the benediction "It is good," but finally, when Adam stood alone, it was not good. God provided the perfect bachelor pad for Adam—all the food he could eat, all the beverages he needed, and all the gold he could spend (Gen. 2:8-14). But it was not good!

A careful search through the animal kingdom failed to find someone who matched him, someone with whom he could talk, share his life, and worship (Gen. 2:19-20). So the divine anesthesiologist put Adam to sleep and performed the first surgery. The result was not a body to be used but a fully equal person to be cherished. Eve was to be Adam's companion, not his plaything.

The translation "helper" for the Hebrew term 'ezer in Genesis 2:18 has justified many a male chauvinist's view that God created women to be Geisha girls for men. The English term *helper,* defined as a "relatively unskilled worker who assists another," lends support to this devaluation of women's status (Webster's, 1971).

I once had a summer job where the hard reality of this definition for "helper" became personal. My job as a carpenter's helper meant that I retrieved tools for my boss, carried boards, listened to his cursing, and occasionally got squirted with tobacco juice when his jaw was full. This is not what God had in mind when He said that Adam needed a helper.

The Hebrew term, 'ezer communicates not inferiority and menial servitude but strength and alliance (BDB, 740). The verb is used approximately eighty times in the Old Testament, often referring to military assistance. And God is usually the one who provides this life-saving aid. Moses, for example, refers to God as his helper, the one who delivered him from the sword of Pharaoh—hardly a weak, inferior role (Ex. 18:4). Three times, Psalm 115 exhorts Israel to depend upon the Lord because He alone is their "help and shield" (115:9-11). When we understand this meaning of helper, no woman should be ashamed to take this role alongside her husband.

Our children need to be taught that the male-female interaction should not be a sex war but an alliance. God originally made man and woman distinct, not to combat one another, but to complete one another. The "oneness" Moses emphasized in Genesis 2:24 was to be far more than the union of two beautiful naked bodies. It was to be the harmony of personalities learning to think, feel, and decide together in reflection of the companionship of the Trinity. This is one of life's richest experiences.

Our present embarrassment concerning sex is symptomatic. We have forgotten to explore who God is, and in turn, we have forgotten that we are made in His image. We have placed our value in ourselves rather than in the One who created us. The loss of our connection with the One in whose image we are made causes us to lose our ability to have healthy relationships. This loss of personal closeness and companionship cools down even the heat of passionate sex.

The Present Embarrassment
Embarrassed about Ourselves: The Search for Identity

So why do we blush about sex? This question is based on a much more foundational one: Why are we embarrassed, even ashamed of ourselves? Our internal convictions about who we are and how much we are worth powerfully determine our sexual beliefs and behavior. Wrong beliefs about sex flow out of wrong beliefs about ourselves. This sex-self connection must be understood if we are to get at the core of what shapes our sexual behavior.

Each of us grows from childhood to adolescence to adulthood searching to find our true worth and a satisfying purpose for being alive. We hunger for importance—to be someone who makes an impact. We crave to get close to others—to experience intimacy. But wrong decisions about what makes us genuinely important and cunning counterfeits of intimate closeness often generate bad choices concerning sex. This in turn breeds increased shame, guilt, and pain.

Reminisce for a moment about the things you lived for in junior high, high school, and college. Sit down with some teenagers and allow them to open up about what is important to them and their peers. We don't need to be Sherlock Holmes to discover that this business of finding ourselves is serious, and deceptions about our physical, personal, and spiritual significance as we grow up in our culture have reached criminal proportions. Wrong choices sexually result from these wrong beliefs about what gives life meaning.

Deceptive Values

I asked a group of students to fill in the rest of the statement, "I am valuable if_____." I tried to discover how their value systems changed from junior high to high school, and from high school to college by prodding them to think back and respond to the statement at these different periods in their lives. Here's a summary of their responses.

In junior high, guys put athletics at the top of their list, followed closely by physical appearance—their clothes, their hair, and the way they presented themselves. They completed their list of "essentials for importance" with grades, popularity, and money. A few added drugs and alcohol. These priorities expressed what they or their peers lived for.

The junior high girls listed "a boyfriend," preferably a high school "sweetheart," at the top of their list. Makeup was also a high priority. Grades, the right group of friends, and school activities, like band and athletics, came next. Permissive parents who allowed them freedom and treated them more like adults were valuable commodities for some of the girls.

In high school, fast cars, mature women, music, and parties moved onto the list of the guys' priorities. The girls added fashion, cheerleading, a college boyfriend, and exciting weekend activities to the usual important items like grades and less restrictions from parents. A job generating some funds became a necessity to help pay for car insurance. An element of cynicism and rebellion crept into their value system with answers like "no curfew" and "beat the system."

College brought needs for more money, the prestige of getting into the right university, and the hunt for an apartment. The guys coveted the high-end vehicles while the girls began to think about a career, engagement, marriage, and a family.

In spite of all the talk about the "teen generation" and the distinctiveness of their

A life without lasting intimacy and impact is empty.

25

world versus the world of adults, underneath the external differences of clothes and jargon, I discovered that the next generation sought meaning from the same idols as adults. Physical ability and looks, intelligence, peer acceptance, money, success, an intense craving for bodily pleasures—these goals mirror the cravings of both young and old. The toys become more sophisticated, the games more demanding, the academics more challenging, and the money more necessary, but the pursuit of meaning remains the same—"If we only had this, or could only do that, or could only go there—then we would be happy!"

Cynicism and rebellion stem from the fact that when children grow to attain a few of their dreams, they are disappointed. The accomplishments fail to deliver. The high schoolers mock what the junior high student believes is "life and death," forgetting that they thought the same thing two years earlier. The college freshman who wears his high school letter jacket is a joke. Our attainments vaporize before our eyes.

As we move from teenager to young adult to older adult we behave like gamers who won't be satisfied unless they reach the next level. We keep pushing the buttons and watching the screen, hoping that the next "life" game will make us feel important and loved. We keep coming up with the wrong answers—cheap products that break and lose their value over time. A life without lasting intimacy and impact is empty.

These embarrassments can make us feel painfully insecure and worthless. Athletics, academics, or other achievements never give us the right answer to the question, Who am I? Why am I important? Three thousand years ago, the author of Ecclesiastes told the truth about pursuing life under the sun —"Utterly meaningless! Everything is meaningless" (Eccl 1:1 trans. mine). Young people and adults with this sense of emptiness become prime targets for sexual exploitation. The boredom of achieving worthless objectives breeds the passion for illicit relationships. Sex becomes another wrong answer to the quest for fulfillment. Sexual sin is an ego problem—the failure to arrive at the right answer concerning one's personal worth. Immorality only intensifies embarrassment about ourselves. But the Creator continues to come to us with the right solution to the question of personal value. He wants us to remove the cheap price tags and place His value on our own lives and our children's—"Made in the Image of God." This is the foundational lesson in our quest for more meaningful, secure sex.

Those raised in homes where the value of life is discovered in personalness, in deep companionship, and in the joyful acceptance of the physical body as a good gift from a generous Creator have a fortress from which they can fight the assault against their sexual morality. God built human beings for intimacy, and His plans offer the most secure way to the fulfillment of these dreams. The next generation and adults made in the image of God do not need to be ashamed of themselves. They do not need to be lonely. Eve conquered Adam's aloneness, and personal companionship in marriage can meet our relationship needs too. But Adam and Eve were not only to enjoy each other's company—they were also to make an impact on God's creation. What was this important role God had planned for them, and for us?

Chapter 2

The Fulfilling Purpose

In chapter 1, we exposed the sex-self connection. Adam and Eve were not ashamed of themselves because their personalities mirrored the ultimate Person in the universe. This legitimate self-worth, rooted in God's worth, enabled them to be naked before each other without embarrassment. The freedom to be intimate flowed from the deep personalness and goodness of their Creator. But God created them for more than intimate oneness. They were destined for greatness as God's appointed rulers over the earth.

Destined to Rule

> God blessed them and said to them, "Be fruitful and increase in number; fill the earth and subdue it. Rule over the fish of the sea and the birds of the air and over every living creature that moves on the ground." (Gen. 1:28)

Hardly a vindictive, begrudging landlord, God commanded Adam and Eve to make love and produce children. Their family's multiplication would give rise to nations that would settle the earth. Adam and Eve and their children were to enjoy the prestigious position of being God's administrative heads over all the earth. Animals were to be subject to their authority, and nature was to give them pleasure. Talk about a confidence builder! Psalm 8 presents this divine job description for humankind, saying, "You made him ruler over the works of your hands; you put everything under his feet" (8:6). This was not a mandate to rape the earth but to order and use it for the Creator's honor, according to His will. His ultimate plan was for human beings to rule the planet, but Genesis 2 reveals that God, like most wise developers, began with a pilot program to test his prospective leader.

Designed for Gardening

> ... there was no man to work the ground...The **Lord** God
> took the man and put him in the Garden of Eden to work it and
> take care of it. (Gen. 2:5, 15)

If I ask you to name some power professions, titles like doctor, lawyer, and CEO probably come to mind. If I ask you to think of persons who serve God, the titles change to minister, priest, and rabbi. Who would ever think of a gardener as a powerful person in God's service? Yet Genesis 2 reveals that humankind's first vocation was not the prestigious medical or legal professions but the simplicity of gardening.

Adam, the divinely ordained gardener of Eden, brings a major misconception to light. We think serving God and worshiping Him involve special titles, holy times, and reverent religious ceremonies set apart from everyday life. Black suits, robes, stained glass windows, awesome cathedrals, majestic pipe organs—these all seem more spiritual than soiled hands, tilled rows, manure, seeds, and crops. But this secular-sacred distinction banishes God from daily life.

In the Old Testament, God did command priests to serve Him in unique dress and through elaborate ceremonies (Num. 3:7-8; 4:23-24, 26), but the first time He used the basic word for worship, *'abad,* He used it for tilling the dirt of Eden, not for burning incense in a temple. *Shamar,* meaning "to keep, guard, take care of," is the second Hebrew verb used to describe humankind's responsibility in Genesis 2:15 (Cassuto, 122-123). And though it later stressed humankind's need to pay careful attention to the obligations of God's covenant (Gen. 18:19; Ex. 20:6; Lev. 18:23; Deut. 26:16), it first referred to the practical task of looking after the Garden (Gen. 2:15).

We presume to confine God in some sacred compartment of life, but He wants us to serve Him in even the mundane tasks. We scratch and claw to achieve power and influence by competing for the prestigious positions, but God says it begins with obedience in the simple tasks of taking care of a garden. When we exclude Him from Monday morning and fail to obey Him in daily responsibilities, a vacuum grows in our lives. Illicit sex can rush into this void.

The ego that drives us to believe we will be important if we become the CEO before we are forty, if we build the biggest church in our denomination, or if we gain national prestige and fame, also drives us into bed with the wrong partner when our accomplishments fail to make us feel important. The stress on success fuels false love.

So beyond the sex-self connection there arises an important sex-power allure when we view wrongly our

> God comes to us like a suitor asking for a woman's hand - with freedom and tenderness, not force.

purpose and priorities. God's man and woman need to discern this sex-power connection and resist its seductive power grab by resting in the satisfaction that true impact comes from closeness to God, not from closeness to the pinnacles of power. Satisfaction with God safeguards moral purity.

God's assigned task for Adam in the Garden was not difficult; neither was the test concerning the forbidden fruit. But the implications of his failure were profound.

Tested by Love

> *The Lord God commanded the man, "You are free to eat from any tree in the garden; but you must not eat from the tree of the knowledge of good and evil, for when you eat of it you will surely die." (Gen. 2:16-17)*

Through the centuries God has taken much abuse over the one prohibition in the Garden of Eden. Fallen human nature intrinsically believes that negatives are bad and blames its failures on God. The truth is that God was the model father who exercised loving discipline in a perfect way.

31

Skillful discipline begins by stressing the positive— *"You are free to eat from any tree in the garden."* It then sets forth the negative simply and clearly and leaves no room for misunderstanding in relation to the disciplinary action God would take if Adam and Eve broke the command—*"but you must not eat from the tree of the knowledge of good and evil, for when you eat of it you will surely die"* (Gen. 2:17).

Demonstrate your love, give simple clear commands, state the consequences of disobedience strongly—all of us can learn from the Heavenly Father's wise example. But with all the Bible's stress upon God's goodness and generosity, why did He have to include one needling negative? Because He made us in His image, and this image included the freedom to choose.

God created us for relationship with Himself, and there can be no intimacy with puppets. Healthy relationships respect the individual's freedom of choice; even the all-powerful God gave Adam and Eve the freedom to walk away. Every husband who remembers proposing to his wife knows this is a prerequisite of love. You must make yourself vulnerable, openly pour out your heart, and risk rejection.

I still vividly remember the afternoon when I asked Mary to marry me.

We had already told each other, "I love you," and had indirectly spoken of marriage. But I had not yet popped the big question and given her a ring. We drove to Letchworth State Park, the miniature grand canyon of Western New York where I made her walk with me across a perilous train trestle that spanned the ravine so we could find solitude in the woods on the other side. Grabbing her hand I led her deep into the forest, nudged her against a pine tree, forced my forearm against her tender neck and growled, "You will marry me!" Gasping, she coughed out, "Yes."

This is not, of course, the way our commitment of intimacy to one another really began. If you know my wife's Dutch heritage you also know that this arrogant, violent behavior would get me nowhere with her. Instead I had to humble myself, put my personality on the line, and tenderly ask, "Mary, will you marry me?" For there to be love, she needed the freedom to say yes or no to my request. The reason? The

Sovereign Ruler of the universe has designed it so that power cannot force the gift of love. Likewise, God comes to us like a suitor asking for a woman's hand—with freedom and tenderness, not force (Hos. 2:14; Ezek. 16:8).

God's love gave Adam and Eve the choice to trust Him or to walk away from Him. He is good, and His test of love was good. The fruit of one common tree in the midst of the Garden provided the test to see if the parents of the human race would freely choose to believe in His generosity and choose to submit to Him, or if they would decide that they knew better about what was good and choose to reject His prohibition. Would they choose to believe that life was found in obedient subjection to His design or in self-centered independence? That was the question!

There was nothing magical or poisonous about the forbidden fruit. Contrary to myth, it was not a symbol for the illicit joys of sexual intercourse. God's command to be fruitful and multiply hardly restricted sexual pleasure. The fruit was not intrinsically evil. All it provided was an opportunity to see whether humankind would choose to satisfy their passion to eat within the limits of God's will or whether they would satisfy their appetite independent of the Designer. This remains the essence of the choice we face in our moral decisions.

True intimacy respects the individual's freedom to choose, for companionship depends upon it. Tragically our immoral hearts, like Adam's, lead us away from God. We easily believe the lie that God is not the giver of lasting pleasure, that we can find the good experiences of life by walking away from humble submission to God's moral parameters. In chapter 4, we will discover how this basic doubt concerning the goodness of God, the root of all sin, instigated the first revolt against Him.

God intended for us to rule, but this rule was to be the expression of close companionship with Himself and humble submission to His desires. World dominion was God's plan, but when Adam chose a path to the throne that led away from God, power became the force of abuse and death. Sex was not immune to this chaotic distortion of God's original design.

Jesus Christ wants to lead us back to the Garden—back to the proper exercise of power in obedience to His Father. When our most basic needs for companionship are met in God, and when our life's purpose is to obey Him in the everyday things, we can find true intimacy and impact. Sex ceases to be another false quest to feel loved and important. We escape the destruction of using sex as a substitute for intimacy or power. We are then free to discover the sacred celebration of sex in marriage. God commanded Adam and Eve to produce a lot of children, but He designed husbands and wives to fit together physically for far more than procreation. What was the sacred meaning of making love in Eden?

Chapter 3
The Sacred Meaning

When I walked into our room after class one afternoon, and my high school roommate was throwing darts at the wall, I knew there was trouble. When a closer look revealed that he was throwing darts at his girlfriend's pictures, I knew there was a crisis in their relationship. Ordinarily, he defended these pictures from all the teasing and ridicule boys in a boarding school could hurl against a young man's first love. Those pictures represented this love, and they held the place of honor in our room. Now he was destroying them. Why?

The relationship was over. His closeness with this girl had terminated. Turning away from her produced the anger and chaos that caused him to hurl darts at her pictures, puncturing and tearing what he now hated.

Though Satan was never jilted by God, he behaves like it. He irrationally chose to turn away from God's throne and His love. Unlike a teen lover who will probably mature and recognize the childishness of his behavior, Lucifer, the archangel, has become the embodiment of deceit, hate, and murder. He throws his darts at every expression of genuine intimacy found in God's creation. The physical unity of two who were to become one in the Garden of Eden, picturing the mystery of the Three who are One, was a genuine intimacy, and God's archenemy hated both the symbol and the reality. Marital intercourse continues to illustrate physically these spiritual realities today; thus, Satan hurls his animosity against human sex. This exposes the evil force behind the filthy jokes, the grotesque graffiti on bathroom walls, the bruises on abused women, and the sexual molestation of so many murder victims. Satan is immoral and vicious. He vindictively drags God's sacred picture of love through the filth of his kingdom of darkness.

So why did God design Adam and Eve in their nakedness to fit together in the first place? Our Creator's response to this question involves more than reproduction. The Author of art and media delights in fleshing out invisible realities in visible object lessons. Human sexuality in marriage is His object lesson to help us begin to learn the wonder of the invisible Triune God. What do we mean when we speak in the marriage ceremony of the "two who become one" in reflection of the "Three who are One"? How does marital intercourse illustrate a mysterious reality about the true God?

The Three Who Are One—Illustrating the Trinity

Those of us raised in the Christian church have heard the standard illustrations to explain how three can be one. Consider an egg, for example—it has a shell, a white albumen, and the yellow yoke, yet it is one. In fact, all this illustrates is that one thing can have three sections—hardly the essence of what the biblical account reveals about God as three persons: Father, Son, and Holy Spirit, forever united in the one divine essence. Perhaps water provides a more accurate example.

Water is one substance that can be a solid, a liquid, and a gas. In fact, at the triple point, it can exist in the gaseous, liquid, and solid phases—all in equilibrium. Doesn't this give us a legitimate model to grapple with the meaning of the Trinity?

Water does demonstrate that one substance can take three different forms, yet, instead of illustrating the biblical teaching concerning God's essence, this object lesson in fact teaches a heresy called modalism—the belief that God is one person who reveals Himself in three different forms of activity.

What we need is an analogy that will combine the two essential realities of the self-revelation of God as Trinity—the distinctiveness of the three divine persons and their unity as the one eternal divine being—*"Hear, O Israel: The Lord our God, the Lord is one"* (Deut. 6:4). I would suggest that Genesis 1 and 2 implies that the union of two distinct persons, husband and wife, in the oneness of marital intercourse presents an illustration that combines these essentials of the teaching concerning the Trinity—the distinction of persons, the equality of their value, and the oneness of their being. This is why marital intercourse is such a powerful picture of the Trinity because both the husband and the wife maintain their personhood but they form a new oneness.

The Two Who Become One

God created the man in his image, in the image of God he created him; male and female He created them. (Gen. 1:27)

This is now bone of my bones and flesh of my flesh;
she shall be called 'woman,' for she was taken out of man."
For this reason a man will leave his father and mother and be united to his wife, and they will become one flesh.
(Gen. 2:23-24)

Marriage liturgies and love songs speak of the need for the two to become one. The beauty of the "two who become one" according to Genesis 1:27 and 2:24 is that it reflects the reality of the ultimate "Three who are One." Stop and ponder the significance of seeing human sexuality in marriage as an analogy illustrating the Trinity. The sacredness of sex as a picture of the Trinity begins to explain the intensity of the struggle that rages in human hearts over this entire issue of sexuality. Sex is not simply a physical or emotional issue—it is an intensely spiritual one.

Twice Genesis 1:27 speaks of God's creating the singular man in His image, yet this man is spoken of as two distinct persons—male and female. Similarly, God speaks of Himself in this context as a plurality, *"Let us make man ..."* (Gen. 1:26a), but also as the one God, *"And God said ... "* (Gen. 1:24). John Sailhammer exposes the connection between the plurality and oneness of God and its reflection in humankind as male and female. He writes, "Following this clue the divine plurality expressed in v. 26 is seen as an anticipation of the human plurality of the man and woman, thus casting the human relationship between the man and woman in the role of reflecting God's own personal relationship with himself" (Sailhamer, 38).

Cornelius Plantinga, in his discussion concerning the Trinity, writes, "Although there is no precise human parallel, theirs is a unity somewhat like a marriage (cf. Gen. 2:24)" (Craigie and Wilson, 916).

My point is that the sexual oneness between a husband and wife is sacred because it reflects the ultimate oneness between God the Father, the Son, and the Holy Spirit. Marital love is an object lesson illustrating the Trinity.

Notice that the unity in a plurality of persons is stressed at the end of Genesis 2. Moses brings his focus on the creation of man and woman to a close with Eve's creation out of Adam as a distinct person who thinks, feels, and decides, and yet she is one with him—"bone of his bones and flesh of his flesh." Moses claimed that this explains the reason for marriage. Marital intercourse causes two distinct persons, a male and a female, who have publicly left their parents' homes and made a commitment to stick together like glue to become physically one. Their sexual union expresses a deeper personal union of thinking together, feeling together, and deciding together, and ultimately, this personal oneness pictures the ultimate spiritual intimacy among the divine persons of the Creator.

The analogy must not be pushed too far. Sexuality must never be viewed as an attribute of the divine being. In chapter 5, we will see that this was the critical error of the fertility religions. So while carefully omitting sex from the godhead, we have discovered how Genesis 1 and 2 does present making love in marriage as a sacred, physical picture that points hearts toward the wonder and mystery of the three divine persons who are forever companions in the essential oneness of the godhead. Therefore, marital sex is not sinful. It is not even neutral. It is sacred. This explains why the Devil detests it.

Adam and Eve stood naked before one another without guilt because their value—made in the image of the King of the Universe—had not been ravaged by selfish pride and rebellion. They were companions, allies, unashamed to be inside of one another because their union would point to the ultimate eternal union in God. From this vantage point, marital intercourse becomes a celebration of intimacy between husband and wife and, with God, an act of joyful worship.

Human history too soon became a tragedy instead of a romance as the idyllic wonder of Edenic nakedness was lost in the shameful rebellion of Genesis 3. A deadly snake, who hated God and the human beings made in His image, invaded the Garden. What were the darts he hurled against Adam and Eve that plunged their race into guilt? How has Satan desecrated the holy image of human sexuality and turned it into an abominable idol? These are the questions we address in part two.

Part Two

Satan's Counterfeit Design

The eyes of both of them were opened, and they realized they were naked, so they sewed fig leaves together and made coverings for themselves.

Genesis 3:7

Chapter 4

Satanic Strategies for Seduction

Contrary to much popular opinion about Adam and Eve's Garden experience, S-E-X was not the forbidden "apple" that plunged the human race into misery and death. However, the lies that caused Adam and Eve to eat the forbidden fruit are the same ones the Snake employs to entice us and our children to indulge in sexual immorality today. And the inevitable price for succumbing to his attack remains the same—death.

Our Adversary, though cunning, is not very creative. Satan continues to use his same tried and effective strategies of temptation. There is no need to be naive about the attacks he will use against us. We must make "Satanic Strategies for Seduction" an essential section in our sex education curriculum. Our Heavenly Father wants to teach His children far more than the biological use of their sex organs or the deadliness of STDs. He intends to give us the knowledge and power to overcome the deadly deceit within.

The Deadly Snake

*The serpent was more crafty than any of the wild animals the **Lord** God had made.* (Gen. 3:1)

To understand what has happened to humankind's unblushing innocence since Eden, we must meet God's archrival—Satan. His name means "adversary," and opposing all that is good and true is the core of this demonic being. If we innocently believe that human temptation, including sexual temptation, involves only instinctual drives seeking immediate fulfillment, we will sorely underestimate the potency of our enemy's venom.

The Bible exposes a source of evil, a supernatural personality, who detests human beings. Like a bloodthirsty man-eater, he prowls

(1 Pet. 5:8). This former archangel, fallen from the throne room of God, appears on the pages of Scripture for the first time not as an angel of light but in disguise as one of the good creatures the covenant Lord of Israel had made—the serpent.

Men and women admire and fear snakes. Their beautiful colors, mysterious legless motion, and deadly strike have made them the object of worship from the beginning of time. Egyptians bowed before Wadjet, the cobra goddess, a special symbol of wisdom, fertility, and healing (Oakes and Gahlin, 297). Ancient myths from diverse locations such as Sumer, India, Anatolia, Mesopotamia, and Greece told the tale of a repressive serpentine monster in the prehistoric past, defeated in a great cosmic war by a heroic god (Waltke, 1-18). The result? The forces of life broke away from the clutches of chaos, and earth became inhabitable.

Genesis 3, in contrast to this idolatry and mythology, does not present an irresistible goddess or mythological fire-breathing dragon as the embodiment of evil. Instead the serpent in the Garden is simply one of the creatures that God made to be subservient to humankind (Gen. 1:28; 2:20). The last book of the Scriptures tears away his mask and informs us that the creature speaking from the body of this serpent was more than a reptile. He was the initiator and first cause of evil itself—the Devil (Rev. 2:9; 20:2).

The pride of modern theologians, psychologists, and sociologists in the twentieth century mocked a religious belief in a personal devil, but the horror of Auschwitz and the killing fields of Cambodia shook this confidence. These bloody horrors testify to a supernatural virulence in evil that biological or psychological mechanisms can not fully explain. Psychiatrist M. Scott Peck challenges his colleagues to develop a "psychology of evil." He answers whether or not Satan exists by saying, "I now know Satan is real. I have met it. . . . Although intangible and immaterial, it has a personality, a true being" (Peck, 183, 209). With police departments forced to have specialists trained in the facts of occult criminal activity, the reality of Satan has suddenly come back into vogue. But who is this enemy, and where did he come from?

In contrast to the imagination of folklore, God's revelation answers the question concerning the origin of evil guardedly. Two classic passages speaking of the rise and fall of two heinous reichs, Babylon and Tyre, transcend their poetic description of two earthly rulers and attribute experiences to them not possible for any human kings.

The prophets Ezekiel and Isaiah disclose hints of a rebellion in heaven in which a wise, beautiful angel, created by God to be one of the guardians of His throne, unexplainably chose to pridefully initiate an insurrection against His Creator. Ezekiel writes,

You were anointed as a guardian cherub, for so I ordained you. You were on the holy mount of God; you walked among the fiery stones. You were blameless in your ways from the day you were created till wickedness was found in you.
(Ezek. 28:14-15)

This defrocked angel is the monster behind all the tyrannical attempts by humankind to rule this world independent from its Creator. (see Rev. 12-13)

Our Creator is light and in Him is no darkness at all (1 John 1:5b). The goodness of our Heavenly Father is never soiled by even a smidgen of moral filth. All that He creates is good. Therefore, He did not cause the malignant wickedness that began to grow in Satan's heart. Nothing explains this spontaneous generation of evil inside one of God's servants! Why an angel chose to become the adversary, or why human beings, whom God created upright, chose to follow their own schemes remains hidden. The consequences are not. The addictive, obsessive, compulsive, and self-destructive behaviors involving drugs, alcohol, food, and sex openly prove human beings are in bondage to a tyranny that defies explanation (Eccl. 7:29).

I believe the lack of an explanation for the origin of evil confronts us with one of its fundamental properties—it is irrational. Sin makes no sense. Unlike a syphilis bacteria that can be identified and annihilated, sin is a humanly untreatable moral AIDS. We must never think we can study and observe its characteristics, explain its origin and history of development, and then come up with a psychological vaccine to control and prevent it. We must reckon with the facts about evil. It is senseless foolishness, the antithesis of life, truth, goodness, and beauty. We must humbly open ourselves to the truth about the evil that dwells deep within each of us.

Jesus teaches that this anti-god foolishness began in the Devil himself. Though He did not explain the reason for this satanic horror and its invasion into God's good creation, Jesus did diagnose for us the basic character of evil. It has not changed from the beginning in the Garden of Eden. Satan still lies and murders (John 8:44).

Genesis 3 never pulled back the curtain of eternity past to explain Satan's origin, but it did lift the curtain on the Garden scene and allow us to listen to the cunning lies he told Eve. We must listen carefully, for he continues to whisper these same half-truths in our ears. Though the origin of evil remains a mystery, we can learn the dynamics of how this chaos seeks to control our lives and resist it.

The Snake Attack

The serpent . . . said to the woman, "Did God really say, 'You must not eat from any tree in the garden'?" (Gen. 3:1b)

Doubt God's Goodness

The serpent's cunning reveals itself immediately. Without directly mentioning God's prohibition, he rivets Eve's attention on the one forbidden thing. The implication behind Satan's half question/half exclamation is that God's restriction is bad. The freedom to eat all the fruit of the trees of the Garden, including the Tree of Life, are forgotten as Eve's understanding of God's goodness begins to fade. Sin is always conceived in the womb of doubt concerning God's good intentions toward us.

As we apply this fundamental satanic trick to sexual temptation, we begin to understand how Satan drowns out the joyful anticipation of marital sex and focuses our attention on God's prohibition of sexual intercourse outside of the marriage bond. Traditional moral scruples are portrayed as the rigid response of a puritanical father who resents the maturing, youthful virility he sees in his children. This doubt about God's good intentions toward us is tragically part of the fabric of our minds. We are all Adam's children. This is why we must turn away from his example and follow the example of our Heavenly Father.

Remember Genesis 2 when God stressed His goodness and humankind's freedom to enjoy? He did not preach only the negative. The Heavenly Father began His training by underscoring the positive. Teaching about sexuality must begin here as well.

One summer I partnered with a skillful musician at a Christian camp. I taught the Bible, and he moved us to exalt our Lord in song. His wife was unable to be with him, and during his concert one evening, while introducing a song, he blurted out, "Man, I miss my wife!" The kids started laughing, and he responded, "That's right. Marital sex is out of this world. God's even blessed us with a child!"

The old school gets red and moans loudly over this blatant reference to sex. Wagging their fingers, they say, "Don't tell them about the intoxication of married love! All that sex talk will make them impatient. They'll be sneaking out and doing it in the bushes." Actually, the opposite is the case. God's sexual instruction extols the thrill of sex in marriage. He doesn't keep this from us; He uses it as His argument for abstaining from sex outside of marriage (Prov. 5:15-23). My friend's spontaneous praise for sex with his wife was healthy and scriptural. May his tribe increase!

We must teach our children that their bodies, including their sex organs, are not bad but good gifts from their loving Creator. The marvelous changes of puberty need to be celebrated as a major step toward adulthood with the responsibility to learn God's purposes for sexuality. Sexual thoughts, dreams, and desires are part of the good creation God has made. Like all potent forces, they must be treated with care and according to the instructions of their Designer. Our children must get the message that God is good, and His creation is good, and though the Devil can produce electrifying sensations, he cannot deliver lasting, satisfying sex.

Add to God's Prohibitions

The woman said to the serpent, "We may eat fruit from the trees in the garden, but God did say, You must not eat fruit from the tree that is in the middle of the garden, and you must not touch it, or you will die." (Gen. 3:2-3)

God's command to Adam said nothing about the location of the tree or about the danger of touching it. Eve's additions to God's law focused on the one restriction. She became blind to all the fruit God had given her.

Legalism believes that the best way to please God and control the passions within is to make additions to His commands. The argument goes like this: If we make a hedge of human stipulations around God's rules that are more restrictive than what God actually says, and, if we rigidly obey these additions, we can be certain God's rules will be protected. By obeying our human peripheral rules, we are safe against offending the core of God's standards. This was the essence of Pharisaic religion in Jesus' time, and He vehemently exposed its lie.

It turns a loving relationship with a divine Father into an agonizing burden of trying to stay in His favor. It focuses all attention on the things we can't do and flames intense desires to satisfy physical passions. This leads to horribly deceptive reasoning: "Since God has prohibited any normal fulfillment of these physical desires, and yet, I powerfully experience them, I must satisfy these longings by turning away from my Creator and doing it my own way."

The sexual domain of Christianity is filled with peripheral rules not recorded in the Scripture. For example, "No physical contact unless you are engaged or married," is one such rule. First Corinthians 7:1 is used to give biblical support for this regulation, *"It is good for a man not to touch a woman"* (NKJV). Legalists believe we must keep a distance of "six inches" from one another. But is this what Paul had in mind?

The preceding context of 1 Corinthians 6:16-17 makes it clear that Paul is talking about far more than holding hands. The Greek expression, "touch a woman," is actually a euphemism for sexual intercourse. Some of the Corinthians were falsely using the slogan quoted above to prohibit intercourse in marriage, and at the beginning of 1 Corinthians 7, Paul seeks to correct this false teaching. He was not making a statement prohibiting physical contact between the sexes.

If Paul believed that a man must never touch a woman, why did he repeatedly exhort brothers and sisters in Christ to greet one another with a holy kiss, a custom which was not limited to only the same sex in the first century (1 Cor. 16:20; 2 Cor. 13:12; 1 Thess. 5:26)?

The no-physical-contact rule, like other human additions to God's principles, fails to deal with the complexities of human relationships. Different expressions of physical contact convey different meanings. Kissing your great aunt, kissing the homecoming queen at halftime, and kissing your wife while snuggled alone by the fire in your den involve different meanings. The first is a family expression of affection, the second is a social expression of honor, and the third may easily become foreplay for sex. Our culture's failure to understand different types of affectionate expression and its constricting of all physical expressions into the sexual arena is a major spark igniting the explosion of illicit relationships. In chapter 5, The Meaning of Friendship, we will seek to expand the importance of brother-sister affection and explore the question of how to express intimacy in more ways than sexual advances.

Eve's additions to God's commands did not protect her from yielding to temptation. The rabbinic hedge erected around the Mosaic Law did not conquer the uncleanness deep inside of the Pharisees of Christ's day, neither will our religious regulations tame the lion of lust in our hearts. Additions to God's commands only move us farther away from the only reality that can conquer evil—the merciful, tender relationship God desires to have with us. Only closeness with God and firm faith in His goodness toward us can defeat temptation. Legalism quenches the passion of this legitimate relationship and leaves us vulnerable to Satan's second lie.

Deny the Reality of God's Judgment

"You will not surely die," the serpent said to the woman. (Gen. 3:4)

Satan drops the indirect interrogation of God's character and frontally denies the reality of the divine sentence, *"When you eat of it you will surely die"* (Gen. 2:17). All this boils down to the basic question of life: Who tells the truth in the universe—God or Satan?

The designer of sex decrees that incest (Lev. 18:1-18), adultery (Lev. 18:20), homosexuality (Lev. 18:22), bestiality (Lev. 18:23), and fornication (Deut. 22:16-17; cf. Heb. 13:4) are abuses of His gift, against His design. Those who practice these perversions will suffer and die, just as certainly as someone who continually sniffs glue will blow his or her brain.

In different cultures down through the centuries, Satan has repudiated one or more of God's sexual laws. For example, the American culture, though still repulsed by bestiality or incest, has accepted homosexuality

Additions to God's commands only move us farther away from the only reality that can conquer evil.

as an "alternative lifestyle." It becomes a question of a variant sexual identity no different than the differences of skin color, thus a question of "civil rights," not "moral evil." Fornication becomes amoral, as acceptable as taking someone out to eat. At the conclusion of many dates, sex becomes the expected tip for an enjoyable evening on the town.

Today people preen themselves and act sophisticated, free from moral restraint. But consider the consequences— AIDS, broken homes, suicide, unwanted pregnancy, abortion. Who needs a litany of social problems to realize that the cost of immorality is enormous? We struggle simply to pay the health care burden, let alone the emotional and spiritual cost. Yet Satan continues to repeat, "You can disobey God's moral laws with impunity. God's restrictions are confining. He is a kill-joy who hopes to restrain you from discovering the full expression of your humanity. Be true to yourself and fulfill your passions." God still replies, *"The wages of sin is death . . ."* (Rom. 6:23). Who is telling the truth? Life depends on the right response to this question.

Enthrone Yourself as God

> *God knows that when you eat of it your eyes will be opened, and you will be like God, knowing good and evil.* (Gen. 3:5)

A major theme of Genesis 1 and 2 is not only the Creator's omnipotence but also His goodness. Like an artist unveiling His masterpiece, God exclaims after completing His creation, "It is good! It is very good!"

Only the aloneness of Adam was not good, and God created the perfect ally to alleviate this negative. The only rational conclusion anyone could come to is that God is very good! And people are the special recipients of His tender love and care.

In Satan's first words to Eve, we discovered that a question concerning this goodness was his first move toward checkmating her. He concluded his interview by a return to this assault against God's character.

He suggested that God's motivation in prohibiting the tree of the Knowledge of Good and Evil was not to protect them but to keep them in their place. The harmless act of eating a piece of fruit promised freedom from oppression and independence to decide for themselves what was good for them. Why not become a god and determine your own destiny?

Eve's next recorded thought was the first time someone other than God declared what was good. She looked and decided the fruit was *good* to eat (Gen. 3:6). The German commentator, von Rad, summarizes the essence of this final step in Eve's seduction: "For the ancients, the good was not just an idea; the good was what had a good effect; as a result, in this context 'good and evil' should be understood more as what is 'beneficial' and 'salutary' on the one hand, and 'detrimental,' 'damaging' on the other. So the serpent holds out less the prospect of

51

an extension of the capacity of knowledge than the independence that enables a man to decide for himself what will help him or hinder him" (Gerhard von Rad, 89).

Observe the foolishness of Satan's lie that one becomes like God by choosing against Him, that one finds good by walking away from the source of all good, that one discovers life by disobeying the breath of life.

Ironically, God's intention from the beginning was for humankind to be like Him. He created us in His image. He never planned to keep us in some kind of innocent naiveté by withholding information about life from us. His inspired wisdom literature offers us craftiness and skill in the facts of life (Prov. 1).

> ## Sin is always conceived in the womb of doubt concerning God's good intentions toward us.

We learn from the book of Proverbs that the Father's will is not for us to isolate our children from the world or to allow them to seriously scar themselves in the school of hard knocks. Instead, God wants us to give our children the insights into life's realities so that when they go out to the freedom of college or a career, they will be dependent on God, wise to the ways of this world, but innocent of involvement in evil. The fatal lie is to think that God is keeping this knowledge from us, or that skill in living can be found by rejecting the foundation of wisdom.

Jeremiah the prophet, not the serpent, told the truth about the source of knowledge:

> *"Let not the wise man boast of his wisdom or the strong man boast of his strength or the rich man boast of his riches, but let him who boasts boast about this: that he understands and knows me, that I am the Lord, who exercises kindness, justice and righteousness on earth, for in these I delight," declares the Lord.* (Jer. 9:23-24)

Once Satan had firmly planted the seed of doubt about God's goodness and the mental teaser of wondering what it would be like to experience what God forbids, he could leave his victim to the assaults of her own senses and imagination.

The Devil Does Not Make Us Do It!

When the woman saw that the fruit of the tree was good for food and pleasing to the eye, and also desirable for gaining wisdom, she took some and ate it. She also gave some to her husband, who was with her, and he ate it. (Gen. 3:6)

Satan cannot force anyone to sin against their will, and all ancient and modern attempts to deny our responsibility for our actions are wrong. Neither our environment, our genes, nor demons are responsible. Satan is deceptively cunning, but he cannot overwhelm the human will to such an extent that we have no choice in moral decision. Thus the human will, not the demon of lust, is responsible for sexual sin.

Satan planted the seeds in Eve's imagination but she made the decision to reach out, pick the fruit, and eat it, and Adam made the choice to dine with his wife. This physical act of eating the forbidden fruit began in the mental processes of Eve's mind. Sexual sin also begins as a deadly mind game. It begins with the input of the eyes.

Eve could have looked at all the other fruit in the Garden, observed the beauty of God's creation, and picked any of it to her heart and stomach's content. There was nothing wrong with good food, beautiful fruit, or the desire to become more knowledgeable about life. The sin was to covet the one thing God did not desire for her.

A husband can gaze at the nakedness of his wife as she disrobes for him, hunger for the thrill of her body, and revel in the satisfaction of her love. After consummation he can relax in her arms, filled with joy that the Creator of the universe is so unbelievably fun-loving that He created such a unique, pleasurable way for a husband and wife to say, "I love you."

The adolescent boy or grown man drooling over the centerfold of *Playboy* sins, not because a woman's body is intrinsically evil, but because his Creator has not given this woman's body to him. God is not jealously keeping the secrets of a woman's nakedness from him or scolding him for his sexual desires. God wants him to understand reality—lusting after an imaginary dream woman, cosmetically enhanced by an artist, is a poisonous substitute for the true experience of giving your body to a real woman who can be trusted because she has committed herself to being your companion for life.

In our culture our young women need to be taught the same lessons as they too face the bombardment of erotic images of gorgeous men seeking to arouse their lust. We need to help both our sons and daughters understand that when our eyes continually feast upon forbidden fruit, they lose their taste for, and enjoyment of, the legitimate fruit. Too often in marital counseling, I have faced the anguish of a wife who can never give her husband what he wants physically, because it is impossible to compete with the "phantom girl" in his head. Satan laughs as a man salivates over a farce and scorns what should be his own private fountain of satisfaction.

Fathers need to talk to their sons about these distinctions the first time they observe their eyes beginning to fight the battle over whether or not to look the second time at a beautiful female body. When a dad and mom find the swimsuit issue of *Sports Illustrated* under their twelve-year-old son's bed, or when their eleven-year-old daughter wants to go to Victoria Secret with some of her older friends, this doesn't call for a sermon against sexuality. It's time for a heart-to-heart talk about God's good plans concerning sexuality and the need to allow Him to control the lust of our eyes. The covetous desire to look at what God does not desire for us, to meet the physical drives of our bodies apart from the design of our Creator, and to justify all of it as our legitimate quest to experience our humanity to the full was not only Eve's problem, it is our struggle too. The Apostle John labels all this—"lust of the flesh," "lust of the eyes," and "pride of life"—the "world," the satanic system insanely committed to rebelling against God (1 John 2:15-16 NKJV).

The Divine Sentence of Death

To the woman he said, "I will greatly increase your pains in childbearing; with pain you will give birth to children. Your desire will be for your husband, and he will rule over you."

To Adam he said, "Because you listened to your wife and ate from the tree about which I commanded you, 'You must not eat of it,'

Cursed is the ground because of you; through painful toil you will eat of it all the days of your life.

It will produce thorns and thistles for you, and you will eat the plants of the field.

By the sweat of your brow you will eat food until you return to the ground, since from it you were taken; for dust you are and to dust you will return." (Gen. 3:16-19)

The Devil uncharacteristically spoke the truth when he told Eve that her eyes would be opened and she would experience new realities (Gen. 3:5). He failed to tell her the rest of the story. When we open our eyes to experiences God prohibits, we discover shame, concealment, blame, pain, alienation, and death.

Sin's invasion into the human race brought a sudden end to the trust between a man and a woman. The reality of their guilt caused Adam and Eve to cover their nakedness and protect themselves from the threat of the new enemy at their sides. Though nude beaches and pornographic movies try to ignore the need for clothes and the dangers of exposure, they are as ineffective as Adam and Eve's skimpy fig leaves at dealing with the distrust sin brings. Only God's cure for genuine guilt and obedience to His design for sex in marriage can begin to restore the trust in one another that makes it safe to take off your clothes.

Satan was right about God's judgment—Eve did not drop dead the moment she ate the fruit. But death is more than the cessation of our physical body. It is alienation from the source of life. After their sin, when Adam and Eve heard the voice of God in the Garden, they hid among the trees. This is death—to hide from the Voice who gives life.

Instead of confessing our guilt, we blame others, and ultimately God, for the catastrophe.

Adam blamed Eve, then turned on God. Wasn't He the One who thought Adam needed a partner (Gen. 3:12)? Denial of personal guilt and transference of blame emerged full grown in the human personality long before Sigmund Freud analyzed personality dynamics. Sin was far more than animal instinct—it was conscious treachery against the Creator.

God's fatherly blessing to Adam and Eve was to fill the earth with their children and to feed them from the abundance of the earth's produce. Sin altered what was supposed to be a great happiness—the birth of children and the cultivation of the Garden—and caused it to become painful, threatening labor. The pregnant woman would labor in pain to give birth to her children, and the man would labor in sweat to feed them.

The cooperative alliance of a husband and wife became the battle of the sexes the instant Adam and Eve chose to be their own god. Observe how the serpent addresses Eve, instead of Adam in Genesis 3:1. Adam, God's ordained leader in this family, is not even mentioned until Genesis 3:6, "*She also gave some to her husband . . . and he ate it.*" By becoming Adam's leader, Eve, whom God designed to be a competent ally to her husband, became his executioner. Satan turned the Architect's leadership model for the family upside down as Eve eased into the controls over Adam. Note that when God entered the scene He immediately addressed Adam and held him responsible for the actions of his family (Gen. 3:9; cf. Rom. 5:12ff).

Genesis 3:16 reveals that the destructive competition between husband and wife over who will rule the home is part of the curse of sin. Genesis 4:7 gives us a clue to the meaning of the word *desire* that God used in Genesis 3:16. It is not a wife's sexual desire toward her husband but the hunger to dominate. Genesis often recounts the sad results when a husband passively allows his wife to assume leadership in the home (Gen. 16, 27, 30). Even the evangelical world has entered the debate over gender identity, and some argue for egalitarian marriage where sexual distinctions are blurred and male leadership is a curse. But consider the consequences when Sarah became the leader over Abraham (Gen. 16), or when Rebecca and Jacob seized the reigns from blind old Isaac: anger, broken homes, pain (Gen. 27).

Because of sin the specter of our body lying in a box, decaying into meaningless dust, terrorizes our dreams and sucks the vitality out of our days. The climax of sexual intercourse makes a man and woman forget this ghost and feel alive. Those who have no confidence of life beyond the last breath deify the mysterious power of sex and other sensual experiences. Faithfulness, security, and trust will all be sacrificed when dust is all we have to look forward to. The fear of losing life is a major factor in the passion to find life in sex. Finding hope in the truthfulness of God's promise, not in sexual novelties, is the only legitimate remedy to the curse of dying.

The Divine Promise of Victory

The Lord God said to the serpent, " . . . I will put enmity between you and the woman, and between your offspring and hers; he will crush your head, and you will strike his heal." (Gen. 3:14-15)

Genesis uses the natural animosity between women and snakes as an object lesson to talk to us about the most intense war in the universe. God discloses at the beginning of His story that the serpent will eventually "bite the dust" in this conflict.

We have already been introduced to the serpent character in this cosmic drama; the literal snake was the evil dragon, Satan, in disguise, the archenemy of the Creator. Moses gives us the first clue to the tension of the biblical narrative when he describes the conflict between those who will choose to be the serpent's family and those who will be the family of the woman. Moses thickens the plot when he introduces a second mighty character in the drama. He narrows Eve's offspring to one male child when he writes, "He will crush your head" (Gen. 3:15b). Though bitten in the heel, this Savior will mortally wound Satan. But who is the serpent slayer?

Genesis 12, 15, and 17 narrow the field as God adds the details that Abraham's family will be the vehicle for bringing blessing again to the nations. Second Samuel 7:16 reveals further that one of David's sons will rightfully assume the Creator's original purpose for humankind as ruler of the earth. Luke 3 gathers the Old Testament hints emphasizing the presence of Adam, Abraham, and David in Jesus' family tree. Allan Ross brings together all the clues and solves the most important biblical riddle concerning the identity of the one who will bring to justice the murderer in the Garden:

The motifs of chapter 3—death, toil, sweat, thorns, the tree, the struggle, and the seed—all were later traced to Christ. He is the other Adam, who became the curse, who sweat great drops of blood in bitter agony, who wore a crown of thorns, who was hanged on a tree until He was dead, and who was placed in the dust of death. *(The Bible Knowledge Commentary: Old Testament, 32)*

But the ironic twist in God's story written in history was that the curse of death could not hold His Son. Jesus rose on the third day defeating death and the Devil by taking the deadly punishment for our sin and offering to give the gift of life and blessing to all who would believe Him. He is the sacrifice who provides the robes of righteousness that forever replace the skins that never could cover Adam and Eve's shame. He comes to each of our hearts today and asks the ancient question again: Who will you trust? The Savior or the Serpent?

The history of the Old Testament reveals the news— many chose to trust themselves and forget God's promise. They kneeled before the creation instead of the Creator. Sex was the name of the goddess human beings adored. And she still reigns in many lives today. But how did Satan distort God's original design, and what characterizes the idol of satanic sexuality?

Chapter 5

Satanic Sexuality

The essence of sin is to reject God's kindness and to assert that we can find what is good by meeting our cravings in ways that pridefully ignore the Creator's blueprints. "Gratify self" replaces "glorify God" as life's motto. Passion enthrones herself as lord over our lives. The sacred purpose of sexuality—the enjoyment of oneness in remembrance of the eternal oneness of the Trinity—is replaced by the heat to compete and dominate. Man's rebellion turns sex from a picture of the Trinity into a dirty joke. Satan's worst obscenity is to push men and women down on their knees at the shrine of the goddess of lust.

Christians bow before Jesus Christ as the true center of devotion and seek to follow His example and teaching. Satan seeks to remove Christ from this central position of adoration in Christianity and to replace Him with a false devotion to sexual experience and other idols. The Bible reveals the origin and nature of this false faith.

The Beginnings of Satanic Sexuality

As the Genesis record walks with Adam and Eve out of God's Garden into the world of independence, it does not take long to expose how their tragic choice ravaged human sexuality. Lamech, the seventh from Adam, in the murderous line of Cain, shattered the divine ordinance of monogamous marriage. From the meaning of his wives' names, *Adah,* "ornament" or "pretty," and *Zillah,* "shade" or "tinkling," it is not difficult to surmise what motivated Lamech to become the first bigamist (Wenham, 112). A pretty face. A seductive voice. A curvy figure. He decided that two toys were better than one. For men apart from God, a lifetime of faithfulness to one partner became an impossible, unnatural ideal. They began to look for multiple relationships with gorgeous faces and bodies, forgetting that women were people created in the image of God. Fornication, polygamy, and concubinage became society's norm.

Lamech's "Sword Song," composed for his two beauties, boasts of his vengeful execution of a young man. Instead of forgiving seventy times seven, Lamech made his enemies pay seventy times seven. Sex and the sword ruled in human culture as the sex-blood connection revealed itself for the first time in the violent line of Cain. Those who live for physical highs soon realize that murder yields some of

> **The sin was to covet the one thing God did not desire for her.**

the most scintillating experiences (Gen. 4:23-24). With the account of Noah and his sons, the history of Genesis goes on to expose another heinous combination—the alcohol-immorality connection (Gen. 9:20-22; cf. Hab. 2:15).

Instead of covering Noah, naked and drunk, Ham went and mocked his dad before his brothers. In contrast to this blatant disrespect, Shem and Japheth backed into the tent and threw a cloak over their father, never gazing upon his shameful condition. When Noah awoke he pronounced a curse, not against Ham, which we would expect, but against Canaan, Ham's youngest son (Gen. 9:25). Is this a case of injustice where *"the fathers eat sour grapes, and the children's teeth are set on edge"* (Ezek. 18:2)?

Ezekiel answers this question with an emphatic, "No!" The righteous judge of the universe tries each individual fairly according to his own behavior—*"The soul who sins is the one who will die"* (Ezek. 18:20). Then why did Noah curse the descendants of Canaan?

Ham's disrespect of parents and his sexual laxity were reproduced in Canaan, his son. Moral laxity, drunkenness, and violence became the characteristic behavior of his descendants, the Canaanites. They became Israel's worst enemies, not from military assault, but from immoral infiltration.

The rape of Jacob's daughter, Dinah, gives us an early glimpse of sexual standards in Canaanite territory (Gen. 34). An unaccompanied, young single girl was never safe. She was fair game for any virile young man.

The Rape

Dinah's breasts swelled under her tunic, and her charcoal make-up made her eyes dark and mysterious. She was now a teenager—old enough to go out with her friends and experience life in the city. Shechem would hardly qualify as a metropolis, but, for a shepherd's daughter, it was big time. When a young prince, important enough to have the city named after him, made his move on Dinah, she was swept into immorality.

Jacob should have known from his grandfather's fears concerning the sexual practices of the Egyptians (Gen. 12:15) and his own father's concerns about the Philistines (Gen. 26:7) that an unmarried woman in town was a target. But like many passive fathers, he remained silent when Dinah pushed for the opportunity to spend some time in the city with the Canaanite kids. His apathetic lack of protection exposed his daughter to a situation that was too hot to handle.

Genesis 34:2 presents the tragic results. He *"saw her, he took her and violated her."* Unlike David's son, Amnon, who after incestuously destroying Tamar's virginity was repulsed by her and threw her out (2 Sam. 13), Shechem, the Canaanite prince, wanted to make his impetuous sex act right. He decided to marry the girl. Tenderly he spoke to her and sought to atone for his illicit penetration of her body and soul. He loved her and begged his dad to make marriage arrangements with her dad.

Shechem never considered how his Canaanite sexuality reversed the divine order of the Creator expressed in Genesis 2:24. Instead of "leave," "be united," and "become one flesh," the Canaanite prince went to bed first, then fell in love, and finally tried to work out a deal for a legitimate marriage. This Canaanite order seems to be the norm for contemporary couples.

When counseling some engaged couples about the "first night," it becomes obvious from their facial expressions that the nervousness about a new experience has long since disappeared. Like Shechem and Dinah, sex comes before the public promise to live together for a lifetime. Though labeled an antiquated hangover from the Victorian Age, a public commitment, not sexual intercourse, is the best beginning point for a marriage. The Creator's order still makes better sense.

In chapter 6, we will discuss the kind of self-controlled love that should mark the beginning of our relationships with the opposite sex.

Shechem's negotiations with Dinah's father and family revealed a vast difference between Canaanite morality and the sexual values of God's people. Neither Hamor, Shechem's father, nor Shechem, himself, apologized or asked forgiveness for robbing Jacob's daughter of her virginity. All they could talk about was the material advantages of a marriage. But Dinah's brothers were furious.

Materialism and sex were the essence of the gods of Canaan even at this early period. When these gods rule, cruel violence is not far behind. The fury of Dinah's brothers moved them to deceitfully use the sacred symbol of circumcision to incapacitate the male population of Shechem's home town. On the third day, Simeon and Levi, Dinah's brothers, slaughtered the male population. Fornication, anger, and violence joined to compose a macabre dance of death.

Leviticus 18 reveals that by the Mosaic era sexual perversions, like incest and bestiality, had become common sexual practices among the Canaanites. By the time of the Israelite conquest, immorality and materialism were enshrined in the temples of Canaan as the state religion. Satan had established his own diabolical perversion of human sexuality. But this deification of sex is not some dusty forgotten part of ancient times. It is becoming a powerful religion in contemporary American society. Canaan exposes its roots.

The Fertility Goddesses of Lust and War

The land bridge at the eastern end of the Mediterranean Sea, between the mighty Egyptian, Hittite, and Mesopotamian Empires, thirsted for seasonal rains and was attacked by desert winds and hungry locusts. The people of Canaan, unlike the Garden of Eden, waged continuous war against drought, famine, and starvation. Human infertility, miscarriages, high infant mortality, and the carnage of war reduced life expectancy in ancient Canaan to thirty-five years of age. Instead of crying out to the God of creation, who originally blessed the earth with fertility (Gen. 1:1ff), the Canaanites prayed to the fertility gods imported from Babylon.

Numerous nude figurines with exaggerated breasts and pudenda from the Canaanite period give archeological testimony that sex had become Canaan's "savior," the source of bread and protection from the threat of death.

The Myth of Baal and the Goddess

Throughout the Ancient Near East the seasons of nature and the fertility of the land became linked to a magical myth of dying and rising deities. In Canaan, Baal, the great storm god, rose to rule the gods as the source of life-giving rain. Texts from the Canaanite city of Ugarit tell his story.

After a victorious combat against the chaotic water-god, Yam Nahar, Baal is given the gift of a beautiful mansion. But at a banquet given by the gods in his honor, he refuses to submit to the demands of Mot, the god of death. Mot swallows his opponent, and Baal slides down his hungry gullet into the netherworld of the dead. Through the cold lifelessness of winter, the result of Baal's imprisonment, Anath, his sister, searches for her deceased brother. Eventually she finds his prison and attacks Mot to secure his release. A revitalized Baal joins in the slaying of death, and through his resurrection and intercourse with the goddess assures the renewal of fertility in the spring (Craigie and Wilson, 99-100).

New Year festivals throughout the Ancient Near East reenacted various forms of this myth. The king played the role of the fertility god and a high priestess would headline as the fertility goddess. Ritual sexual intercourse between the king and the priestess supposedly stirred the male god to plant his seed in the womb of the mother goddess of earth and thus ensure the return of productivity to the fields.

Sexual promiscuity had become an act of worship at Canaanite temples and shrines, which employed male and female prostitutes and provided rooms for sex for those who came for religious services.

These prostitutes were called the "holy ones." All this high energy sex was supposed to stir the agricultural powers of vitality. Yet the true God decreed that this orgiastic revelry brought a curse instead of a blessing on the land (Lev. 18:26-28).

Though Moses condemned these practices, Israel and Judah succumbed to the seducing sensuality of the fertility cult. By the eighth century B.C., the Prophet Hosea had to rebuke Israel's daughters and daughters-in-law for prostituting themselves under the trees at Canaanite high places. He shamed the men for flagrantly consorting with shrine prostitutes. In Hosea 4:12-13, the prophet describes the immoral idolatry of his contemporaries.

They consult a wooden idol and are answered by a stick of wood.
A spirit of prostitution leads them astray; they are unfaithful to their God.
They sacrifice on the mountaintops and burn offerings on the hills, under oak, poplar and terebinth, where the shade is pleasant.
Therefore your daughters turn to prostitution and your daughters-in-law to adultery. (Hos. 4:12-13)

Hosea's report informs us that, as in the Garden of Eden, men and women were in trouble over a forbidden tree. Only this time the tree took the form of a wooden idol, probably carved to represent a male penis (Andersen and Freedman, 366). Hosea uses the same Hebrew term *'es, "tree,"* used by Moses in Genesis (cf. Gen. 3:1, 2, 3, and 8) to refer to the phallus symbol used in Canaanite worship to represent Baal, "the master." The female goddess, Asherah, a Hebrew word meaning "grove," was also sometimes presented as a flourishing tree (Deut. 16:21). Ironically, the seduction of a "tree" was again plunging men and women into ruin.

Instead of listening to God for the answer to life's riddle, they sought revelation from a deaf and dumb piece of wood and the exotic pleasures of sexual perversion. Instead of covering their nakedness with leaves and hiding in the trees as Adam and Eve had done, they now undressed in the shade of the trees and unashamedly engaged in promiscuity.

The true worship of Yahweh in the Old Testament stood in sharp contrast to this false Canaanite cult. The Ark of the Covenant rested at the center of the Holy of Holies in the Jerusalem temple, instead of the sexual symbols of Baal and Astarte. Inside this sacred chest were the stone tablets. One of the laws engraved in stone was, "You shall not commit adultery." The God of Moses defended purity, faithfulness, and the sanctity of the family. The Canaanite cult, in contrast, celebrated Satan's potent brew of intoxicants, magic, and sex—a religion that sought to guarantee the good life. The history of Israel in the Old Testament records the conflict between these two competing systems of belief and the infiltrating power of Canaan.

Sometimes as a confused combination of Yahweh faith and Canaanite worship, sometimes as the bold repudiation of the true God, God's Old Testament people turned away from personal devotion to Him and enthroned the gods and goddesses of lust, materialism, and intoxication. Their true divine king could not be ignored.

The bloody Assyrian destruction of the Northern Kingdom in 722 B.C. and Nebuchadnezzar's butchery against Jerusalem in 586 B.C. demonstrated the murderous consequences of rejecting the Lord God and becoming intoxicated with false gods (2 Kgs. 17:7-12; 24:3-4). When Israel and Judah dethroned the biblical worship of the true God, they forgot that their new queen, the goddess of love, was also the goddess of war. W. F. Albright writes,

> Another dominant characteristic of the Canaanite goddesses in question was their savagery. In Egyptian sources Astarte and Anath are preeminently goddesses of war; a favorite type of representation shows the naked goddess astride a galloping horse and brandishing a weapon in her right hand. In a fragment of the Baal epic which has just been published [1938], Anath appears as incredibly sanguinary. For a reason not yet known she massacres mankind, young and old, from the sea-coast to the rising of the sun, causing heads and hands to fly in all directions. Then she ties heads to her back, hands to

her girdle, and wades up to her knees—yes, up to her throat—in human gore. The favorite animals of the Canaanite goddess were the lion, because of its ferocity, and the serpent and the dove, because of their reported fecundity. (Albright, 233-34)

Drunkenness, immorality, and violence—they feed one another. Thus, we discover that human sacrifice was also a ritual in the Canaanite cult (2 Kgs. 3:27). Is this deification of immorality and violence forgotten among the crumbled stone altars of ancient Canaanite cult centers and the ruin of the ancient Israelite monarchy? Tragically the story of sex worship continued. In Carthage, before Rome's rise to power, children were placed in the outstretched arms of a bronze idol. A fire burned behind and below the statue and the children would fall into the flames and be consumed (Ringgren, 162). Thus, the human sacrifice practices of Canaan invaded Northern Africa.

During the Hellenistic period, between the Old and New Testaments, the goddesses Anath and Astarte blended together into a single figure—the Syrian Atargatis. Her cult was famous for its "galli," devotees who voluntarily castrated themselves for the goddess and thereafter dressed as women *(Encyclopedia Britannica,* 968).

By the first century A.D., the Apostle Paul exposed the Gentile culture as sexually impure, degraded, "indecent," "arrogant," "heartless," and "ruthless." He penetrated to the root cause of all this vile passion—humankind had suppressed the truth about God, the Creator, by his enjoyment of wickedness. Instead of respecting divine power and thanking God for His goodness, people perpetuated the error of Genesis 3 and installed themselves as gods (Rom. 1:18-32). This error continues today.

Our god is whoever or whatever we believe can make life meaningful at any given moment. When we reject the true God, the intense cravings of our physical bodies lobby for lordship over our lives. The sexual experience with its powerful magnetism, driving heartbeat, pulsating push into the generative organs of life itself, union with another naked body, and explosion of desire can easily become the goddess of choice. Men and women will sacrifice everything for the one moment of ecstasy.

Scott Turow concludes his best-selling novel, *Presumed Innocent,* with a gripping testimony from Rozat K. Sabich, his novel's lead character, who exposes the power and religious fervor of this illicit passion within.

Rozat is a bright deputy district attorney in a major metropolis, trapped on a broken rung of the political ladder. His affair with Carolyn Polhemus, herself a successful lawyer who specializes in prosecuting sex offenders, leads to her gruesome death, to his trial for her murder, and to the near destruction of his legal career. His marriage disintegrates, and he is separated from Nat, the young son he loves. Reminiscing about these tragic events and his involvement with the illicit love that led to all this brokenness, he concludes,

> I reached for Carolyn. In a part of me, I knew my gesture was ill-fated. I must have recognized her troubled vanity, the poverty of feeling that reduced her soul. I must have known that what she offered was only the grandest of illusions. But still I fell for that legend she had made up about herself. The glory. The glamour. The courage. All her determined grace. To fly above this obscure world of anguish, this black universe of pain! For me there will always be that struggle to escape the darkness. I reached for Carolyn. I adored her, as the faith healer is adored by the halt and lame. But I wanted with wild, wild abandon, with a surging, defiant, emboldened desire, I wanted the extreme—the exultation, the passion and the moment, the fire, the light. I reached for Carolyn.
> In hope. Hope. Everlasting hope.
> (Turow, 421)

Listen carefully to the religious terminology— "escape the darkness," "faith healer," "exultation," "light," "everlasting hope"— yet this religion worships sex, not the true God. This cult crushes life instead of saving it, leads to death, not everlasting life. Hope is strangled. And when sex is deified, she becomes impotent. The intensity of her experience wanes with time. Different techniques and positions, multiple sex partners, homosexual and lesbian sex, bestiality—nothing can satisfy the cravings. Paul warns us that all this is not valid worship but the vicious addictive slavery of burning lust. Like most addictions this is a journey into death (Rom. 1:24-27).

Teenagers sexually giving themselves to each other in the afternoon before their parents come home from work, singles in a sensuous "lambada" frenzy at the latest night spot, businessmen, with cocktail in hand, drooling over partially clad bodies of striptease artists; homosexuals engaging in multiple sex acts in a single night; middle-aged husbands forsaking their brides for a last tango with a young beauty; thousands buying tickets to see the latest sex king and queen burn hot in bed—all these are the modern manifestations of Satan's ancient fertility cult.

A teenage girl committing suicide when her boyfriend breaks up with her, a drunken fist fight late Saturday night outside a club, an AIDS victim gasping to hold off the onslaught of pneumonia, a middle-aged wife suffering from a nervous breakdown committed to the psychiatric ward, a husband shooting his wife and himself after receiving divorce papers, millions of dead unborn children—this barrage of daily news warns us that the same intoxication-immorality-violence connection is still at work in the modern satanic counterfeit. This explains why the intensity of sex and violence provides the standard by which modern critics rate our entertainment. What is the root of our addiction to sex? Why will we risk everything for a few moments of passion? How can we find a lasting cure?

We must discern that environment, lack of biological information, or social pressure is not the primary cause of sexual problems in our lives and in society. The cure for immorality commands deep, internal devotion—a religious commitment. The only way to defeat the goddess's deadly effect is by falling in love with a moral King who is far more powerful than satanic sexuality. He alone can teach us how to recover the joy of the Garden—how to make love without shame.

Part Three
The Savior's Restoration

"The two will become one flesh." This is a profound mystery— but I am talking about Christ and the church.

Ephesians 5:31-32

Chapter 6

The Meaning of Love

Sandra was obviously troubled as she came into her pastor's study. A sophomore in college majoring in elementary education, her personality usually bubbled with enthusiasm. But this afternoon her eyes were strained—a pain coming from deep inside. The introductory small talk gave her some moments to muster her courage and begin to expose her reason for the appointment.

"You know that Matt and I are planning to get married in two months. We've already contacted you about beginning our premarital counseling in preparation for the ceremony. But I needed to talk to you alone without Matt. Matt and I have been together for five years, since my sophomore year in high school. He's the only guy I've ever seriously dated, and I think I know him, but I'm frightened.

"You've taught us that marriage is for keeps, and when I make the marriage vows, I intend to keep them. That's why I want to be sure I'm making them to the right man. When we started going together, I was sure Matt was right. He was good looking, an excellent student, and faithfully attended our church youth group. When he asked me out for a date, I was concerned about my parent's reaction, but they were thrilled. They even encouraged me to spend time with Matt, and I enjoyed it.

"It was nice not having to worry about whether I would have a date after a Friday night game or on the weekend. He was always there to talk to in between classes or in the cafeteria during lunch. Before I knew it, we were officially together. He would get mad if another guy even looked at me funny. I was flattered by Matt's intense jealousy. We were paired off for the rest of high school, spending all our spare hours together. It was comfortable, secure, and expected.

"Matt still swears he loves me, but how do I know if it's the real thing? Sometimes, I find myself dreaming about what it would be like to date some of the guys I'm meeting at college. After class, I've had some good casual conversations with a few of them. I talk more freely with them than I do with Matt. Is there something wrong with me?"

Sandra needed some tissue as she fought the tears that began to form. Her pastor pointed to a box on his desk and used the interruption to throw out his advice.

"Why don't you tell Matt you need some time to be sure? You think it would be best to slow down the marriage plans and give both of you some space to date around. If you two genuinely love each other, it won't take long to find out."

Sandra's response caught him off guard. "I can't slow down our relationship. How could I go out with another guy? You don't understand. No, Matt and I have not gone all the way. We agreed early in our dating that premarital intercourse was a sin, but we've done everything short of the sex act. I've given too much of myself to Matt. I've got to marry him."

Matt and Sandra represent another couple who entered their relationship through the door of sexual love. Though they attended church regularly and confessed that Jesus Christ died for their sins and rose again, their dating life was dominated by messing around. These young lovers interpreted the intense physical magnetism they felt for one another as true "love," and the pleasure of this gratification made them feel important and precious to each other. At this stage of adolescence, as their personalities began to develop, how were they to realize that their new discoveries of the intensity of male-female contact and its constant pressure to get close was not love—especially when "love = sex" is the equation in much of our culture?

Cunningly, sexual desire began to make herself god, the source of their life together. But with sex at the center of their relationship, they could not discover the real meaning of love, of friendship, or of sex. What does the Source of Love say about the meaning of love, and where does He believe we should begin this business of relationship with the opposite sex?

True Love

Shakespeare taught us that it happens in a "Midsummer Night's Dream." Hollywood repeats the refrain as it dramatizes the overwhelming moment when eyes meet, bodies tingle, lips touch in silent wonder, and destiny has spoken. Mention L-O-V-E and the rush of a cloud nine romance is cheered as its most authentic expression. This magic euphoria solves life's problems. Ultimate answers are found between the sheets with the most desired sex partner imaginable.

Strangely, when God speaks to us of true love, He takes us not to a bed of pleasure but to the agony of a hill called, "The Skull." There, we witness the ultimate moment of love. It is not in the intensity of pleasure as two naked lovers intertwine, but in the incredible pain as the Eternal Lover hung naked on the tree, stretching out his arms to hug prodigal humanity back to the Heavenly Father: "*This is love: not that we loved God, but that he loved us and sent his Son as an atoning sacrifice for our sins*" (1 John 4:10).

This love is not the mutual satisfaction of one another's ego needs. It is not a surge of neural impulses switching on the pleasure centers of the brain. Neither is it the intellectual satisfaction of knowing you are connecting with another's ideas. Christ's love was a choice of His will that led Him to the ultimate act of love. He obeyed the desire of His Father and sacrificed Himself to take the death penalty for those who detested Him. He willingly remained on the cross in the midst of a crowd as they cursed and yelled, "*You who are going to destroy the temple and build it in three days, save yourself! Come down from the cross, if you are the Son of God!*" (Matt. 27:40).

True love is not competitive; it does not have to prove itself or selfishly meet its own personal needs. It is so secure that it can sacrifice itself to save another. Jesus Christ, knowing that the Father had put all things under His power, gave Himself up for the sake of His enemies (John 13:3; Rom. 5:8).

Adam's rebellion closed the door to love and closeness with our Creator. Christ's obedience paid the just penalty for our rebellion and reopened the door to intimacy with God. In fact, Jesus Himself comes to our door and knocks. If we will listen and let Him inside, He will establish a relationship with us forever (Rev. 3:20).

Our children need to hear this truth. They need to hear it as more than the pious chant of a preacher's Sunday morning routine. We must all go back to the cross like children and allow the price Jesus paid there to melt our pride and teach us to love. The meaning of life is not found in athletics, clothes, popularity, power, money, grades, pleasure, or sex, but in the simple refrain, "Jesus loves me this I know, for the Bible tells me so!" Jesus recaptured God's purpose in creation (Gen. 1:27). He is the perfect image of God, and He desires to recreate this image in us.

> *Do not lie to each other, since you have taken off your old [Adam-like] self with its practices and have put on the new [Christ-like] self, which is being renewed in knowledge in the image of its Creator.* (Col. 3:9-10)

We all listen to the variety of voices in our heads. The instruction of parents and teachers, advice from friends, TV sitcoms and dramas, newspapers, magazines and books—they all fill the channels of our minds. Daily, we decide whose voices we will believe and whose we will reject. Our behavior results from these choices.

When someone hears that Jesus Christ's death paid the penalty for their rebellion against God, when they affirm that He rose again, and when they personally choose to rely upon this Jesus, who lives today, for their destiny, God instantaneously gives them the gift of a new character. His Holy Spirit takes up residence inside their personality and begins to strengthen this newborn spiritual life (John 1:12; Eph. 3:16).

This new birth means more than an emergency exit ramp to heaven when we die. Daily, the Spirit of God wants to straighten out our faulty thinking so that like Christ we may continuously realize that God's will is good and right for us (Rom. 12:2).

We hear His will most clearly in the words of the Bible. Our reading gives us the opportunity for a personal interview with God. We must listen intently and submissively to what He is saying. Reverent respect for Him is the foundation upon which we can build a skillful life (Prov. 1:7). We can begin to see through Satan's lies and live according to truth. Christ's voice needs to rule in our minds. When it does, we progressively become like Him. This, not the experience of pleasure, is life's most important priority; for this is the only way we will escape the deadly bondage of satanic sexuality. Paul puts it like this,

> *The night is nearly over; the day is almost here. So let us put aside the deeds of darkness and put on the armor of light. Let us behave decently, as in the daytime, not in orgies and drunkenness, not in sexual immorality and debauchery, not in dissension and jealousy. Rather, clothe yourselves with the Lord Jesus Christ, and do not think about how to gratify the desires of the sinful nature.* (Rom. 13:12-14)

Jesus Christ is the real thing that needs to take the place of the false worship of sex. What all of us want is love, and the Son of God does more than teach us about it. He is love. The evidence that He is in our lives is the love He enables us to show to one another (1 John 4:11-12). This gift is more than words and feelings. It is love in action.

Character Traits of True Love

We search the dictionary to find an intellectual definition of *love,* to put its essence into words. But instead of telling us what it is, God shows us what it is, how love does and does not act. First Corinthians 13:4-7 is Paul's classic description of the identifying characteristics of genuine "Made in Heaven" love. This ought to be the standard for evaluating all our relationships.

1. Love acts patiently.
Love endures the faults and affronts of others—it covers a multitude of sins (1 Pet. 4:8). Love rests in God's ability to forgive and change ourselves and others through the cross of Christ, or, if our enemy refuses to believe in Christ, it leaves the need for righteous vengeance to the justice of God (Rom. 12:17-21).

If Matt and Sandra have found true love, they will be able to be patient with one another. They will not have to rush their marriage, afraid that if they put it off, they will lose their love for one another. Genuine love can be patient.

2. *Love acts in kindness.*

Love graciously helps another, even when it is rejected. God's kindness causes Him to restrain His anger against sin and give us time to turn away from it and toward Him (Rom. 2:4). He does not condemn and judge us (Rom. 8:1); instead He demonstrated His kindness toward us by sending His Son (Titus 3:3-8).

If Matt genuinely loves Sandra, he will continue to be friendly and kind to her, even after she hurts him by putting the brakes on the wedding plans. He will continue to strongly declare his love but will give her the freedom to turn toward or away from him. Love knows it cannot force itself upon another.

3. *Love does not act jealously.*

When love has legitimate exclusive claims, it passionately guards them. For example, God defends the exclusive devotion we owe to Him alone as the one true God (Deut. 32:16). A husband and wife should strongly protect the exclusive relationship they have together. But love does not distrust its partner. It does not burn with envy every time it sees the object of its love giving time to others. Love doesn't attempt to manipulate, control, or stifle the gifts of its ally. It can rejoice in another's success. Love does not claim the right of possession over a man or woman before the sacred marriage vows have been made.

If Matt blows up at Sandra, when she opens up to him about her fear, he is filled with pride, not love. A girl can be overwhelmed with this intensity of passion for her, but she needs to grow up and beware—this is not love but a threatened,

> When we begin to grow in Christ, we learn to allow His death to forgive the sins others have committed against us.

76

insecure ego. In marriage, this jealousy could become a confining prison that robs her of any personal freedom.

4. Love does not brag, it does not pump itself up.

Love, unlike inferiority, does not boast of its superior knowledge (1 Cor. 8:2) or depth of spirituality (1 Cor. 14:37). A friend of mine once warned, "Watch out for the person who constantly tells you how spiritual he is! He is probably lying to you about something else as well." These arrogant people don't have time to love. They are too busy making sure everyone around them knows how great they are.

5. Love does not act disgracefully or rudely.

Love always treats another with dignity and respect. Love has good manners. Paul instructed young men who found themselves being drawn into an intense physical relationship with the woman they had promised to marry to go ahead and marry her so that their mutual physical desires could be satisfied without disgrace (1 Cor. 7:36).

As parents, we must be careful not to push our children toward immorality because we demand too much time for education or financial security before we give them our blessing. Paul believed that marriage was the place to satisfy sexual desires.

Yet in the earlier stages of courting, we need to learn not to allow the physical to overpower our need to get to know a member of the opposite sex as a person. If Matt and Sandra had realized that true love does not act disgracefully, they would not have made physical contact the entrance and foundation of their relationship. This could have given them the opportunity to get to know more than one another's bodies. If the dimensions of self-sacrificial love had been nurtured earlier in the relationship, their physical attraction could have been permitted to build as they drew near the time when they would pledge their lives to each other.

6. Love does not seek its own satisfaction.

The issues important to love are not self-fulfillment, self-justification, or self-pleasure. Love's concern is to meet the needs of others. If eating a particular kind of food offends another's conscience, love does not eat (1 Cor. 10:24). If openly expressing one's beliefs about certain characteristic taboos in a particular group will only generate anger and hurt, love can keep its convictions to itself (Rom. 14:22). Love has higher priorities than what it eats, drinks, or believes about debatable matters. Love's priorities are to obey God's standards, to foster peace and harmony among God's children, and to celebrate the joy of being in Christ's family (Rom. 14:17-18). Love builds others up. Pride tears others down.

If Matt loves Sandra, he can demonstrate it by being concerned about her need to know whether or not he is God's gift to her. He will want her to find peace and strength in this conviction and will rest in the confidence that if Sandra is God's bride for him, He will help her know this in her heart. This does not mean Matt should be nonchalant or *laissez-faire* about the relationship. Love speaks upon a woman's heart as it allows her freedom to make her choice (cf. Hos. 2:14-15).

7. *Love is not easily angered.*

Love does not agitate people until they lose their temper. Love itself is not touchy. It realizes that by living in an unjust world, there will be reason to get justly angry. But love never allows even righteous anger to dominate its thoughts. Anger becomes the acid of internal bitterness when it is stored up. The human mind is the wrong container for this corrosive material. Prolonged anger becomes Satan's toehold into our lives (Eph. 4:26-27).

As a pastor, I am asked by many couples to help resolve some of the issues that threaten their relationships. Finances, in-laws, unfaithfulness, and communication all strain the modern marriage, but I believe unresolved anger is the dominant problem behind the mushroom cloud of devastated nuclear families. Stored anger can explode in an attack of verbal and physical abuse or it can simmer as deep depression. Love does not store angry feelings. It learns how to express intense emotion honestly and constructively. Love speaks the truth in love (Eph. 4:15).

8. Love does not keep a record of wrongs.

Jesus forgave those who crucified Him, and all of us must realize that we are members of this crowd (Luke 23:34; 2 Cor. 5:19). When we respond to Christ, we allow his death to pay the penalty for our personal sins. When we begin to grow in Christ, we learn to allow His death to forgive the sins others have committed against us.

> *Let there be no more bitter resentment or anger, no more shouting or slander, and let there be no bad feeling of any kind among you. Be kind to each other, be compassionate. Be as ready to forgive others as God for Christ's sake has forgiven you.* (Eph. 4:31-32 Phillips)

We must daily take our personal grievances against others to the foot of the cross. There we find personal forgiveness and the reason to forgive others. Love does not keep a mental journal of hurts that deserve repayment. Love throws away the balance sheet.

9. Love never gloats over the moral failures of others.

Love throws a cloak of silence over what is displeasing in another. Love does not relieve boredom by entertaining itself in the scandal sheets of other's lives. Instead, it weeps over the pain wickedness brings. One of the worst forms of depravity is to laugh while others fall. True love gently seeks to restore (Gal. 6:1).

10. Love celebrates when truth triumphs.

Truth creates an atmosphere where love can grow. Judgments and criticisms produce antagonism against others. Gossip (telling the truth about someone to the wrong person at the wrong time) and slander (peddling a ruinous lie about someone) are the poisons that murder friendships and love. Those who love get their facts straight and then never use them to club someone into the ground. Love wants to restore others in truth (Gal. 6:1).

11. *Love perseveres.*

Love is willing to put up with mistreatment and misunderstanding to help others understand and believe the truth. Euphoric romantic highs ebb and flow, but true love, the foundation of a strong marriage, remains steady. This is the strong bond that builds homes where the security of the children's lives is not threatened by every emotional shift between their parents. Genuine love never walks out on a family to follow idealistic dreams of finding the one true romance. This is why both husbands and wives are commanded to love one another (Eph. 5:25, Titus 2:4).

12. *Love believes God and confidently depends upon His promises.*

Paul would never claim that love is naive—wanting to believe the best about everything and gullibly trusting everything it is told. The object of Paul's belief was Christ and all that He said. Because Paul knew God and His purpose, he did not despair when things looked impossible. The faithfulness of God, not childish idealism, gave Paul hope. This is what love believes and what gives it hope.

13. *Love never fails.*

This Christ-like love will stand when all else has fallen. In a world of change, love never wears out. Love will be the atmosphere of heaven forever. God wants us to allow Christ to make love the atmosphere of our lives, our homes, and our churches now. We are commanded to behave like this toward all humankind. This self-sacrifice for others needs to become a circle of love big enough to encompass the entire population of this planet (Matt. 28:19-20).

Paul's words on love from 1 Corinthians 13 are so familiar and clear they can easily be ignored. The pressing urgency in a society that defines love as sex is to make them the standard by which we judge our feelings. All of our relationships, including those between the sexes, need to be evaluated on the basis of this Calvary love. When this all-encompassing circle surrounds our lives, God can give us the joy of a smaller circle of intimacy—brother-sister relationships and friendships. How should these more personal "loves" affect our lives together as males and females?

Sandra broke the heavy news to Matt while they were finishing their lasagna at a nice Italian restaurant. Though the candles continued to burn in the middle of the white tablecloth, the atmosphere was anything but warm and romantic. Matt felt like Sandra had doused him with ice water. He took her home in silence and did not accompany her to her door. Sandra cried alone in her bed. Sleep was impossible. She questioned, "Did I do the right thing? Maybe I said good-bye to my one true love. We might never kiss again!"

Chapter 7

The Meaning of Friendship and Family

Love does not equal sex. It equals self-sacrifice for the good of others. In the last chapter, we learned that we need to reprogram our thinking and understand that when Christ commanded us to "love one another," He was teaching us that a 1 Corinthians 13 kind of love needs to control all our relationships with others. Anything outside the boundaries of these actions is not love, but lust, a deadly part of the satanic sexuality from which Jesus came to deliver us.

Jesus invites us to join Him in declaring His love for the world. But though He ministered to the masses, the Gospels reveal that Jesus had a smaller circle of intimacy—a circle of friends and family. What does His example of friendship with males and females teach us about closeness with others and control over our sexual desires? How can a proper understanding of the brother-sister relationship restrain the destructive power of sexual lust?

A Circle of Friends

In His omniscience, Jesus knew all men, but in His humanness, He chose to narrow His circle of acquaintances to a group of seventy who knew Him well, to twelve who spent hours with Him, to three who were His closest friends, to one who was His best friend. At the transfiguration, when Jesus went up into the high mountain, His three special friends, Peter, James, and John, separated from the rest of the disciples and witnessed His glory. At the last supper, the disciples knew who would lie nearest to Jesus physically, for John was the closest to Jesus personally. The King James Version writes, *"Now there was leaning on Jesus' bosom one of His disciples, whom Jesus loved"* (John 13:23).

Only the intense wickedness of our contemporary culture could interpret John and Jesus' relationship in sexual terms. This attempt to justify homosexual relationships is a diabolical lie. As first century Jews, Jesus and John would die for the teaching of the Mosaic Law. Jesus said Himself, *"I have not come to abolish [the Law or the Prophets] but to fulfill them"* (Matt. 5:17). The thought of disobeying Leviticus 18:22 would nauseate these sons of the Torah. We must allow the true biblical Jesus to teach us about a closeness with others that does not involve sex—closeness built on sharing personal thoughts and plans, not sexual organs.

> *My command is this: Love each other as I have loved you. Greater love has no one than this, that he lay down his life for his friends. You are my friends if you do what I command. I no longer call you servants, because a servant does not know his master's business. Instead, I have called you friends, for everything that I learned from my Father I have made known to you.* (John 15:12-15)

Jesus reveals to us the essence of friendship love—it is companionship, the closeness of allowing someone to know what is happening inside your thoughts. It is conversation about ideas, dreams, and plans. It is letting someone in on your "personal business." This love is rooted not primarily in the will, as are the choices of 1 Corinthians 13 love, but in the union of intellects. Jesus was one leader who did not fear getting close to others. He allowed His disciples to enter into some of the very thoughts of God Himself. Accusations of favoritism did not frighten Him into isolation from others. He spent only thirty-three years on earth, and had the most strategic mission to accomplish in this short lifespan, but He still had time for close friends.

A lack of true friendships is a major cause of the epidemic immorality that plagues our society. Professionals, including pastors, are particularly susceptible. The "old school" taught ministers to avoid close friendships, especially in their own congregations. Others would become jealous, they argued, and this would destroy their effectiveness as a man of God. A strong clergy-laity distinction developed, and ministers were placed high in the pulpit, isolated from others. The power of position intimidated others from taking the risk of approaching their ministers. No one could get close enough to hold them accountable or to provide a confidant to share the enormous burdens of temptation or discouragement.

This "old school" also instructed ministers to avoid close friendships with women. A single pastor was encouraged to find a wife quickly so he could be protected from uncontrollable sexual desires and the gossip that would destroy his ministry. Any physical contact was off limits. Any expression of physical affection was regarded only as sexual.

This teaching made the common error of reducing all male-female relationships to sexual terms. This view never considered the variety of implications of a hug, an arm on the shoulder, or a kiss. Some of the messages expressed by these simple gestures have nothing to do with sex but a lot to do with human companionship and friendship. The sad result of this teaching was to produce a pastor who was stiff and cut off from the kind of physical expressions of warmth that God commands His children to give one another. How does this doctrine align with the examples of Jesus and Paul in the New Testament?

As Jesus moved about, women traveled in His entourage. Two of his closest friends were women: Mary and Martha. As a single man, He frequently enjoyed hospitality in their home. He encouraged them to sit at His feet in the position of a learner of the Torah and listen to His instruction (Luke 10:38-42). When their brother, Lazarus, died, John reminds us that "Jesus loved Martha and her sister" (John 11:5). Jesus jarred the religious prudes of his day by allowing a formerly demon possessed woman, Mary Magdalene, to travel in his party (Luke 8:2).

The Last Temptation of Christ scandalously took this relationship and eroticized it (Scorsese). Again the modern equation "relationship = sex" is a strong testimony for our culture's sick obsession with sexuality. We have difficulty reading about a man and woman being together without concluding that they go to bed together.

The authentic Jesus counters this obscenity and teaches us the rich dimensions of closeness with others based upon accomplishing a job together, sharing together around a table while eating, learning together, or simply having fun together. Jesus enriches all of our lives by His example of intimate friendships. He rebukes our culture's focus upon sex, a focus that robs people of the legitimate joys of companionship and closeness to others.

Jesus enjoyed friendships with both men and women without sexual impropriety. But He was the sinless Son of God, and we are obviously not. How can we keep sexual desires from igniting out of the growing closeness of a friendship? Relishing the freedom to satisfy our hunger pangs for companionship in legitimate forms of friendship is one vital step. Becoming keenly aware of the boundary lines between friendship and sexual attraction is another. We must sensitize ourselves to the little cues that alert us when we cross over from friendship to sexual advance. The closeness of a healthy friendship—the listening, the encouraging, the teaching—must never be betrayed by sexual abuse. We must see illicit sex as treason against the sacred trust of friendship.

Curt, 38, and Janet, 28, met for the first time in beginning Greek class. Curt was the professor, Janet, the student. Curt could not help being impressed with her linguistic quickness and the seriousness with which she attacked the task of learning the skills of exegesis. She already possessed a master's degree in linguistics, had served one term on the mission field, and was now using her furlough to meet her lack of theological training. She was also single and lonely.

Curt had a Ph.D. in biblical studies from a prestigious Ivy League school. His wife, Christine, had worked as a medical receptionist for four years while he finished seminary training. His grades at seminary and the promise that he would return to teach for at least five years provided a grant from his alma mater for doctoral studies. Finally, Christine could take off her receptionist wardrobe and stay home. After only six months as a housewife, she proudly put on a new outfit—maternity clothes. Curt put in fourteen-hour days in the library grinding out his dissertation, but he did find a few moments on the weekend to be with his wife. After four years of the professional school

86

"paper chase," Curt returned to his alma mater to teach, accompanied by his wife and two children, Samuel, 3, and Rebecca, 1-1/2.

Curt's life settled into the routine—battling rush hour traffic to work, teaching five hours of classes, office hours answering student questions, rush hour, home to eat supper, one hour to play with Sam and Becky, children's bedtime, and a stack of papers to grade. Curt hadn't had time to read anything but scholarly theological journals for nine years. He forgot there was a piece of literature called a "novel." Two small children made it difficult to take Christine out to a nice restaurant and the symphony. Curt loved teaching, but life's romance was dying in a hollow predictable routine.

Janet came to his office in the afternoon the first time to ask him to explain the Greek use of the participle. He had lost her in his lecture when he plowed through the section on translating circumstantial participles.

"Dr. Winslow, the Greek participle is going to flunk me. I don't have the foggiest idea what you were saying this morning!"

Curt smiled and reached for a file. "Let me get out my notes, and we'll see if I can do a better job of explaining it this time."

He carefully reviewed the material, and by the quickness of Janet's comprehension, he knew the culprit was not her intelligence but his obtuse communication. After only a half hour she had things down well enough to go to the library and control the rest of the material on her own.

"Thanks for putting up with my silly questions!" "No, that's the reason I'm here! Feel free to come by any time if something isn't clear."

She smiled. Their eyes met, and she left the office. Curt felt strong satisfaction. He was glad he could help Janet along. Teaching became charged with meaning again when he felt like he had been able to encourage a student and equip her for ministry.

Prompted by Curt's invitation, and pressed for time by the number of hours, she was cramming into a couple of semesters, Janet started coming by his office frequently. It was much faster to get a live explanation than to try to figure out the textbook. Her Greek improved, she started calling him by his first name, and they began to talk about a lot more than Greek. They had become friends. Janet shared the agonizing loneliness she felt on her last term while translating deep in the jungle. Curt shared his concern that he would never be able to write for academic journals in his specialty because of his intense course load. He confided his fears over how he could pay for another child on a seminary salary. Christine was six months pregnant, and, to add to the load, she had developed a diabetic condition.

When Janet was in Curt's office one afternoon, the telephone rang. His face turned white. "Christine had to be rushed to the hospital. They're afraid she might miscarry. The emergency room doctors are more concerned about her safety. Her water retention is far too high. She is swelling dangerously."

Janet drove Curt to the hospital in her car. He was far too shaken to drive himself. All they could do on arriving at the hospital was sit in the ICU waiting room and react every time the telephone rang, or another doctor entered the room. Finally Christine's doctor came in at 11:00 p.m. with the news that things had settled down. She and the baby were stable. The danger was subsiding, and they would all have to simply wait. Curt could go home and get a good night's rest. The nurses would call immediately if there were any new developments.

When Curt and Janet arrived at his house, the children had already been farmed out to one of his colleague's homes. Janet offered to come in and fix them something to eat. The moment hit when Curt started to pull the chair out for her to sit down. They stood close as he reached out and his arm brushed hers. She turned toward him.

Their eyes met, and they both knew the sexual energy between them was electric. On receiving the good news about Christine they had spontaneously hugged as a brother and sister, but in this place, at this time, both of them knew that if they got any closer, restraint would be almost impossible. Curt reached out his hand, but not for Janet. Like a gentleman, he pulled out her chair, and she sat down. He went around the dinette table and sat down on a chair across from her.

"I never dreamed a grilled cheese sandwich could look so good. Thanks for driving me to the hospital and for helping me out in all the mess this afternoon. Thanks for your friendship!"

They finished supper, cleaned up the mess, then Janet said good-bye and left. They both knew that they had come to a boundary, were tempted to cross, but chose to remain in legitimate territory. They had not betrayed the beauty of friendship for the treachery of forbidden fruit. Everyone will face times of vulnerability, and the decisions we make in those moments are hugely significant.

Curt thanked God that night for the preciousness of his wife and children. He cried out to His Lord for Christine and the baby's safety. He prayed that he would never betray them by giving himself away to an illicit affair. He thanked God for Janet's friendship and prayed for strength to never betray the trust between them. She was a student, not a prize. More importantly, she was his sister in Christ. They must never forget the sacredness of this spiritual brother-sister relationship made possible through Christ.

Back in her own apartment, Janet asked the Lord for wisdom to beware of settings where temptation could ignite. She prayed for Christine and Curt together as a couple and for their children. She pictured three-year-old Sammy and little Becky in her prayer. She added Christine and Curt's new baby to the family portrait and asked God to protect her from ever destroying this circle.

Purity remembers the sacredness and value of Christ's crucifixion and the spiritual family relationships it generates. Impurity forgets and ignores these priceless values.

The Family Circle

Treat younger men as brothers, older women as mothers, and younger women as sisters, with absolute purity.
(1 Tim. 5:1b-2)

Legalism believes we control our sexual desires with rules against physical contact between the sexes. The Bible knows that the control of lust involves much more than a simple rule—it exhorts us to believe that immorality is the betrayal of precious legitimate relationships. When Timothy faced the threat of immorality, Paul did not give him a rule to withdraw from close relationships with women. Instead he taught him to focus on the importance of the family relationship generated in Christ. All women, except his wife, were to be treated as a mother or as a sister. Learning to relate to the opposite sex as a member of one's family, and not as a sex object, can and will deliver us from the domination of illicit eroticism.

When I speak to teens about dating relationships and open it up for questions, invariably they ask, "If a couple is going together how far do you think it is permissible for them to go in expressing their physical love for each other?"

When the audience is a group of Christian kids, the basic premise behind this question remains the same. Almost anybody with morals and some knowledge of Scripture knows that sexual intercourse outside of marriage is sin. But whether or not it is wrong to engage in the physical actions of kissing, messing around, and the progressive exposure of their bodies to one another is negotiable. Teens are not the only ones who follow this deceitful line of thinking. The teenagers want an authority to tell them where to stop in the process of making love before it becomes dangerous and wrong. What they need is not a stop sign along the road but a totally different route.

Instead of making sexual love the doorway and sustaining force of dating relationships, we must learn to relate to the opposite sex as brothers and sisters. Paul is clear: for a man to treat a woman in ways not appropriate for a brother to treat his sister is impure; for a woman to treat a man in ways not appropriate for a sister to treat her brother is impure (1 Tim. 5:2). There are no exceptions to this principle. Even in a day when incest has raised its ugly head, we still understand the purity and tenderness of the true brother-sister relationship. This model needs to be our guide in dating.

The brother-sister example gives the freedom to get to know one another as persons, not as objects. A guy who goes out on a date and thinks only about when he can start kissing her doesn't even hear the girl say, "I'm into music. I'm glad my mom stayed on me about piano lessons. Do you play a musical instrument?"

The only instrument he wants to play is her body. And if he is thinking erotically, all he hears is, "Can we get away from this group?

Will we be alone? When can the physical contact begin?" The unfulfilled desires of erotic love outside the marriage relationship shout louder and louder making a couple deaf to the kind of conversation that could lead them to know each other as friends, as close brothers and sisters.

Some label Paul's advice as totally unrealistic for the twenty-first century. They assume teenagers will be sexually active; thus, they pass out condoms and explain how to minimize the threat of disease. The tragedy of this advice is that it is not only unsafe physically, but it denies the personhood of these teens. It views them as animals that cannot control their instincts, instead of as men and women made in the image of God. Teens want to be treated as special human beings.

When I ask them about how it hurts them when their mom or dad has an affair, or what kind of faithfulness they expect from their partner when they themselves marry, suddenly sexual control and commitment to purity become high priorities.

Our kids need to know the truth—a twenty-minute ceremony in front of a church is not going to change them morally. If they could not control their sexual desires before marriage, and they went too far with someone they were not married to, there is a strong possibility they will yield to their desires and experiment with an illicit lover after marriage. Satan does not quit on us because we get married. The satisfaction of marital love is God's answer to sexual desire, but it does not cause the battle of illicit desire to end.

A month or two after the wedding a husband can wake up and find that the sleeping beauty he married was the wicked witch in disguise, or a wife can discover that when she kissed her prince, he turned into a slimy frog. At this crucial stage in their marriage, when the idealism of their attraction to one another has crashed, God wants them to begin the hard work of building a solid maturing marriage, but Satan wants to take them back to the courtship days—with another person.

A young wife might find that she has to work to help their marriage get off to a solid financial start. Every morning she gets herself decked out to go into the marketplace to work in the big office. The man she works for is not a struggling, bumbling twenty-four-year-old who is still trying to learn how to handle a woman but a mature, suave six-digit-a-year executive. He starts by taking her to lunch, and then he suggests that she go to his apartment. If the woman has not learned to control her sexuality before marriage and to guard her heart by learning the difference between a brother-sister business relationship and a male-female sexual relationship, there is a strong possibility that unfaithfulness will mar her young marriage.

Erotic love is only safe and satisfying when surrounded by the companionships of the brother-sister relationship and the obedient self-control of Calvary love. The intoxicating freedom of marital intercourse is so precious to our Designer that He composed several exquisite, erotic songs to celebrate it. They are found in the Song of Songs. The Creator's blessing upon marital sex is the subject of our next chapter where we will discover how Christ can lead us on a journey back into His Garden—the Garden of marriage where a husband and wife can again take off their clothes and make love without shame.

Matt didn't contact Sandra for a week after their Italian restaurant confrontation. Then he called. "Sandra, I called our pastor and met up with him. We had a good talk. He shared with me some things about true love and friendship and the need to not enter into a relationship with a woman through the door of sexual desire. I'd like to go back to the beginning in our relationship. This time I want to get to know you as a person. I've got two tickets to the Dallas Mavericks game Friday night and there's a new restaurant in the West End we could try. Would you go out with a guy who wants to be your friend?"

Sandra said yes, and though it took more than a year, Matt and Sandra did eventually say their vows at the altar. This time Sandra was ready for the smallest circle of love. She was unafraid to give herself to the man at the altar who had become her intimate friend.

Chapter 8

The Meaning of Sex

Satan uses sex to destroy human beings by alluring them to bow down before it as an idol. The true divine ruler of heaven and earth curses this deification of sexuality, and, instead, uses marital intercourse as part of His good creation to reaffirm His personal closeness with us. Through Jesus Christ, sex in marriage is not sinful; it is not even neutral. It is a divine command to celebrate the pleasure of God's goodness. Marital intercourse becomes a sacred object lesson of the Trinity and a celebration of God's faithfulness to His vows to us. But the New Testament reveals a new feature in the picture—marital love mirrors the intimacy that exists between Christ and His bride, the church. The thrill of the sexual union reflects the ecstasy the entire universe will experience when Jesus Christ silences the Serpent's rebellion forever.

As we battle with the temptation to abuse our sexuality, part of our armor is the knowledge that our bodies do not belong to us. They are God's sacred temple, purchased by the payment of Christ's life (1 Cor. 6:13-20). Adults and teens must be challenged to understand and to act on the premise that our purpose in life is to please Christ, not to get high on sex. When our bodies honor God and our lives please Christ, He can bring His children through the wide circle of sacrificial love and the smaller circle of friendship into the exclusive oneness of marital love. Then sexual intercourse becomes a second line of defense, God's safeguard against immorality.

After they say "I do" couples need to relax in God's goodness and heed His command to enjoy the legitimate fruit of marriage—freely making love to the glory of God without shame.

The Divine Order to Make Love

> *Since there is so much immorality, each man should have his own wife, and each woman her own husband. The husband should fulfill his marital duty to his wife, and likewise the wife to her husband. The wife's body does not belong to her alone but also to her husband. In the same way, the husband's body does not belong to him alone but also to his wife. Do not deprive each other except by mutual consent and for a time, so that you may devote yourselves to prayer. Then come together again so that Satan will not tempt you because of your lack of self-control.* (1 Cor. 7:2-6)

Though Paul's instructions were too much for many ancient copyists, who changed his command for the husband to meet his wife's needs for sexual intercourse (7:3) to giving her *"the kindness to which she is entitled,"* Paul emphatically stood opposed to the Corinthian ascetic practices of refraining from sex in marriage. He cherished the opportunities his "singleness" provided for unencumbered service to Christ, but he never argued, like Augustine, that sexual passion was a result of the fall of humankind (Saint Augustine, 218). Paul believed that both marriage and singleness were gracious gifts from God (7:7). He recognized that when a believing couple burned with passion to unite sexually, this showed that they had the gift of marriage, not celibacy. In marriage, they should begin a life of meeting one another's sexual needs (7:9).

Satan always maximizes illegitimate relationships and minimizes legitimate ones. The Corinthians fell prey to this deception. They made the false deduction that since they were now a new creation in Christ, their physical bodies no longer mattered. Since sex was material, and they had become spiritual, some concluded that having intercourse with temple prostitutes meant nothing. Paul countered this libertine error with the fact that their bodies had become the sacred dwelling place of the Holy Spirit. To join this temple with sexual immorality defiled the holy place (1 Cor. 6:12-20).

94

Other Corinthians concluded that the normal enjoyment of sex in marriage was sinful. Paul countered this view with his inspired instruction for married couples to fulfill God's original design and beware of false piety that encourages restraint from physical union.

Some mothers and mothers-in-law warn young brides, "Men are animals. You'll have to simply grin and bear their constant desire to use your body!" But Paul counsels husbands first about their responsibility to meet their wife's sexual needs (1 Cor. 7:3). Sexual satisfaction is not the exclusive domain of men. Believing husbands are responsible for the sexual enjoyment of their wives.

Like the lover in the Song of Songs, the husband must remember his wife's delicate view of herself and her body. He must praise her beauty in public before others (1:4b, 9-11; 2:2) and in private to her alone (1:15; 4:1-15). He must remember that his praise is one of the major means the Lord will use to build her sense of value and meaning. The skillful husband follows the example of the wise man of Proverbs and praises his wife in the gates (Prov. 31:28-31). He knows that making love begins not with a touch but with a word of encouragement and thankfulness. This gives his wife the gift of his highest esteem; she possesses his heart.

Paul also reminds each wife that her body does not belong to herself but to her husband. She must give it to him as a gift and meet his sexual needs. Paul's advice to wives reminds us of the uninhibited exposure the Shulammite gave to her husband in "The Dance of the Mahanaim" in the Song of Songs:

> *Why would you gaze on the Shulammite as on the dance of Mahanaim?*
> [The husband's praise of his wife's beauty]
> *How beautiful your sandaled feet, O prince's daughter! Your graceful legs are like jewels, the work of a craftsman's hands. Your navel is a rounded goblet that never lacks blended wine. Your waist is a mound of wheat encircled by lilies. Your breasts are like two fawns, twins of a gazelle. Your neck is like an ivory tower. Your eyes are the pools of Heshbon by the gate of Bath Rabbim. Your nose is like the tower of Lebanon looking toward*

Damascus. Your head crowns you like Mount Carmel. Your hair is like royal tapestry; the king is held captive by its tresses.

How beautiful you are and how pleasing, O love, with your delights! Your stature is like that of the palm, and your breasts like clusters of fruit.

I said, "I will climb the palm tree; I will take hold of its fruit." May your breasts be like the clusters of the vine, the fragrance of your breath like apples, your mouth like the best wine."

[The wife responds]

May the wine go straight to my lover, flowing gently over lips and teeth." (Song of Songs 6:13-7:9)

Here is a wife who knows her husband's male visual fascination with the woman's body. She creatively meets this need by dancing seductively before him. As she rhythmically moves before him in her transparent gown, every line of her exquisite form entrances him. Moving up from her feet to her thighs to her middle to her breasts to her neck to her face to her hair, her poetic husband comments on his delight in every part of her body. Aroused, he pictures the foreplay leading to intercourse as climbing a graceful palm. He caresses her breasts as though picking the fruit of the date palm, her kisses bring him pleasure as the finest wine, and the fragrance of her breath carries the scent of apple blossoms. Never obscene, but powerfully erotic, the ancient metaphors for love still move us to celebrate the wonder and power of sexual love.

Though "religious sensibilities" continue to keep these sections of God's Word from being taught, the "all Scripture is God-breathed" of 2 Timothy 3:16 includes this sensuous dance of the Song of Songs. We must learn how to artistically appreciate the beauty of the human body and to relish its delights in the marital relationship. The lack of artistic appreciation and expression in evangelical circles is another factor in the epidemic of immorality. Song of Songs points the way to art and to moral sexual pleasure.

In view of America's stress upon using the right sexual techniques to achieve the ultimate personal satisfaction, we need to learn from Paul's and Solomon's inspired sex education. When the bedroom becomes a laboratory and partners begin to seek the ultimate climax and orgasm, sex is again elevated to the level of goddess—providing the ultimate value to our lives. God never intended for sex to occupy this blasphemous position.

Paul's advice shatters this selfish obsession as he counsels the husband to yield his body to his wife. He is to use it to meet her needs. He advises the wife to submit her body to her husband's pleasure. They should lose themselves in each other as they seek to bring joy and pleasure to their partner. The primary focus is not on a personal high but on the ecstasy they can give to one another. Ironically this is the path to the greatest sexual satisfaction—a satisfaction that does not wear out over time.

Personal sexual fulfillment, like happiness, is something we experience while we lose ourselves in someone else. When we press to find personal happiness, it always eludes us. When we are not looking for it but become totally absorbed in something else, suddenly, it dawns on us, "I'm happy!" The husband and wife who follow Paul's advice and become absorbed in giving the gift of sexual pleasure to their lover will suddenly discover that God has given them the gift of personal sexual fulfillment (1 Cor. 7:3-4; cf. Prov. 5:15-23).

A Time to Refrain from Sex

When a couple's ultimate goal is to please Christ there can be strategic times when they mutually decide to refrain from sexual intercourse. Physical problems can gently counsel marriage partners not to make love. If intercourse generates pain, a couple is wise to consult a physician or counselor and determine if there is some physical or emotional cause for the discomfort. Intense spiritual needs can also demand the need for abstinence for devotion to conversation with God. This decision must be mutual and caution must be exercised about the extent of the abstention.

Though recognizing there is a time for couples not to embrace in intercourse, Paul argues against anyone who would seek to make a prolonged abstinence a spiritual good. Paul felt so strongly about the need for married couples to make love that he labeled it "robbery" to abstain. To cease from love-making too long is to spurn God's provision for sexual desire and exposes the couple to the danger of a satanic attack. He will try to use their sexual hunger to entice them into the arms of an illicit lover (1 Cor. 7:5).

Does sex in marriage serve only the negative function of protecting couples from immorality? Did Paul and the Scripture only look upon it as a divine safeguard against sin? Illicit sex was the question Paul faced in 1 Corinthians 7, but his letter to the Ephesians answers the positive question, What does it mean for a husband and wife to make love in Christ? Here we recapture the profound meaning and sacredness of marital love.

The Mirror of Christ's Love for His Bride, the Church

> *Husbands, love your wives, just as Christ loved the church and gave himself up for her to make her holy, cleansing her by the washing with water through the word, and to present her to himself as a radiant church, without stain or wrinkle or any other blemish, but holy and blameless. In this same way, husbands ought to love their wives as their own bodies. He who loves his wife loves himself. After all, no one ever hated his own body, but he feeds and cares for it, just as Christ does the church—for we are members of his body. "For this reason a man will leave his father and mother and be united to his wife, and the two will become one flesh." This is a profound mystery—but I am talking about Christ and the church. However, each one of you also must love his wife as he loves himself, and the wife must respect her husband.* (Eph. 5:25-33)

Here for the first time, the three circles of love—unselfish giving, personal sharing, and sexual union—all come together in the husband-wife picture of Christ's love for His church. Paul demolishes the immoral myth of Canaanite sexuality by replacing its lurid gods and goddesses with the true revelation of the Son of God entering into a covenant of love with those who accept the forgiveness offered through Calvary. Sexual intercourse is not included as a literal part of this spiritual intimacy, but it physically illustrates for us the mysterious invisible oneness we enjoy with Christ. One day, when the world of eternity becomes our home, we will discover that this invisible relationship was the true lasting reality.

The Heavenly Reality

Like God the Father in the imagery of Ezekiel 16, the Son of God is pictured in Ephesians 5 as finding a young, undeserving woman with a sordid past with whom He falls in love. He takes this rejected, immoral woman and gently bathes her, clothes her in royal apparel, and makes her his queen (cf. Ezek. 16:9-14 with Eph. 5:26). He proves His love by the gift of His life to set His beloved free. Thus, the Messiah Jesus, not Oedipus, Don Juan, or Tom Cruise, is the source, inspiration, standard, and promise of true love. The vow of this eternal lover will be kept for eternity, "My death in your place and your response to my word is the cleansing bath that can internally wash away your sin." He heals the diseases and removes the blemishes of his bride's immorality and sin (cf. Rom. 1-3; Eph. 4:17-19), and she is destined to become His radiant bride. The imagery of a romantic love story becomes the powerful portrayal of Christ's love for us on the cross and in the resurrection, and a picture of His maturing work in our lives as He prepares us to live in His presence in heaven. He is now in the process of preparing His bride for the wedding (cf. Eph. 5:26-27).

Our physical marriages are meant to point the way to this far greater love story of eternity. The significance of this spiritual drama of love causes the battle of our marriages to become intense. Satan hates God's physical illustration of spiritual reality. In the wedding ceremony, when I give my pastoral charge to the couple, I remind them that only Jesus' love can sustain the meaning of their marriage.

"Your union and covenant today will establish a new relationship. Jesus builds relationships that last, that are built on the gospel. He wants you to illustrate His love for His church, which He gave his life for."

All these thoughts of Christ's death, of cleansing, of forgiveness of sins, of consummation in heaven, of living with Him forever, take us into the theological stratosphere. How does all this relate to our marriages on planet earth now and the meaning of making physical love in the present?

The Physical Illustration

Paul comes back down to earth and argues that the husband needs to love his wife because she is part of his body just as believers are part of Christ's body. She must therefore receive the same tender care and provision a man naturally gives himself. In sexual union, their bodies do literally join. The husband must not forget his union with her after she leaves his embrace and they go out into everyday life. Their physical union should represent a much more profound spiritual and personal union of their personalities with Christ and each other. Personal withdrawal and isolation from her detracts from this reality.

Our union with Christ and our union in marriage do not obliterate the individuality of our distinct personalities but create a new unity of companionship and closeness to another. Paul points us back to what we learned in Genesis about the ultimate oneness, yet continued distinctiveness, between the persons of the Trinity. The husband and wife remain individuals, but their love joins them together into the dynamic oneness of companionship, a oneness that points to their eternal union with the Savior. We find intimacy and companionship in love with a Savior who is there forever.

The exhilarating "one flesh" intimacy between a husband and wife is one of God's assurances that separation, pain, and death will not be His final chapter written about our lives. In Christ we are heading toward ultimate loving and sharing in the joyous celebration of God's family forever (see Markus Barth's discussion in *The Anchor Bible,* vol. 2, "Ephesians," 641).

The Foretaste of Eternal Pleasures

Few recognize that the ecstatic pleasure of marital love is a tender reminder that our Creator is good and a reassuring comfort that agonizing pain will not have the last word in His universe.

"I will betroth you to me forever; I will betroth
you in righteousness and justice, in love and compassion. I will
betroth you in faithfulness, and you will acknowledge the LORD.
"In that day I will respond," declares the Lord—"I will
respond to the skies, and they will respond to the earth, and the
earth will respond to the grain, the new wine and oil, and they
will respond to Jezreel. I will plant her for myself in the land; I
will show my love to the one I called 'Not my loved one.' I will say
to those called 'Not my people,' 'You are my people'; and they will
say, 'You are my God.'" (Hos. 2:19-23)

Hosea used the Canaanite myth of the marriage of the gods but replaced an immoral god and goddess with the God of Sinai and His covenant people. The purity and loyalty of a monogamous marriage replaced the manipulative immorality of the fertility cult. God the Creator pictured Himself as Israel's legitimate husband and Israel as his loved wife.

Hosea 2:19-23 brings us the sweet ending to the prophet's bitter romantic account of God's relationship with His people.

Unfaithfulness, attempts at restoration, divorce, judgment, death— God's marriage to His people turned into a chaotic tragedy. But God proclaimed that this mess of broken promises, illicit loves, judgment and death would not be the last chapter of His love for His bride. He is the keeper of promises, the only reliable Lord who can save her from unfaithfulness.

Like a young lover, He woos His fallen former wife into the wilderness alone where He can speak to her tenderly (Hos. 2:14). He gives her gifts and finally wins her heart. She responds to Him in a miracle of love. His wedding present is the gift of His personal character infused into the personality of His bride. She, who willfully broke His moral commands, would now be righteous. Her heart, which spurned His love, would now beat passionately for Him (Hos. 2:19-20).

In the phrase "you shall know the Lord " (2:20b NKJV), Hosea uses the language of sexual union as a metaphor to picture God's future oneness with His people. The verb "to know" in Hebrew has strong sexual connotations and is often used of a man having intercourse with a woman (Gen. 4:1; 24:16; 1 Sam. 1:19 NKJV). The setting of Hosea 2:20 is a marriage feast—the gifts are given, the celebration begins, and the lovers are expected to consummate the marriage. Hosea does not shrink back from using a term to describe this consummation of God's love for Israel that likened God's love to a husband having sex with his wife. The prophet did, however, delicately switch from the first person account with Yahweh speaking directly, to the third person, "You shall know the LORD." This again cautions us against making sexual relations part of the literal activities of God. Sex remains a valid part of God's creation but not a part of His being. It is a metaphor, a symbol of the eternal closeness and exhilarating pleasure we will experience in the future consummation of the kingdom of God.

Hosea, like Paul in Romans 8, pictures a future day when the curse against nature will be nullified and death will be vanquished. All creation will sing and dance at the joy of God's union with His redeemed people.

The exquisite delights of sex in marriage are a harbinger of the celebration when…

…the dwelling of God is with men, and he will live with them. They will be his people, and God himself will be with them and be their God. He will wipe every tear from their eyes. There will be no more death or mourning or crying or pain for the old order of things has passed away. (Rev. 21:3-4).

The Designer who implemented such an intoxicating and pleasurable means for a husband and wife to communicate their love can be counted on to fulfill His promise of an eternal future free from pain and death. Married love celebrates this vision of a new heaven and a new earth when Jesus' prayer to His Father will be answered affirmatively *"that all of them may be one, Father, just as you are in me and I am in you. May they also be in us so that the world may believe that you have sent me"* (John 17:21).

Married sexual love is therefore sacred, as it illustrates the mysteries of the Trinity, of Christ's relationship with His church, and of our future confidence of intimacy in the Creator's family forever.

But what of those who have taken this beautiful picture and dragged it through the mud of sexual immorality? Is there hope for the naive teen who committed fornication before she hardly knew what sex was about, for the playboy who tried to prove his manhood by conquering women, for the divorcee who tried to ease her loneliness in a series of casual affairs, or for the preacher who railed against sex in the pulpit but became ensnared in the bed of a prostitute? Can the Savior cleanse the filth of satanic immorality and make a man or woman morally pure again?

Part Four

The Joyful Sound of Forgiveness

Brothers, if someone is caught in a sin, you who are spiritual should restore him gently. But watch yourself, or you also may be tempted. Carry each other's burdens, and in this way you will fulfill the law of Christ.

Galatians 6:1-2

Chapter 9

The Anatomy of Adultery and Murder

A phone call at 2:00 in the morning sent terror through Pastor Lewis's soul. Had one of his church members been involved in an accident? Perhaps a heart attack had sent one of his people to the emergency room? The sound of his oldest son's voice calmed his fears for a brief moment, then shocked him like death. "Dad, I'm sorry, sorry to call so late. Our church board meeting just ended. I had to resign my pastorate. I've been unfaithful to Melissa. Can you and Mom ever forgive me?"

Michael was his father's pride. Straight As through high school and college, attendance at the seminary where he had graduated, building his first church from twenty to four hundred in four years—George Lewis's fellow pastors heard the glowing reports. But a few brief words in a late-night call were all it took to shatter the success story.

The media covers every detail of the fall of a superstar pastor or evangelist, but there would be no newscasts concerning this fall of a small-town pastor—only his wife's angry emptiness, his father's paralyzing grief, and his own despair that his sin was vocationally unpardonable.

Michael's father had taught him the biblical values of sexuality. He had learned the Scriptures in seminary and had even taught moral purity to teens and adults. How could he have committed sexual treason against God and against his wife? Did his sin forever disqualify him from a position of leadership in the church?

The secular world seduces its citizens to sin, applauding those who escape detection and stomping on those who get caught. Lance Armstrong made millions as a celebrity athlete and swore he didn't take drugs, but when it proved to be a lie, the public turned against him. Magazines like *Texas Monthly* debate whether or not he should be forgiven. The bigger question for all of us is, "Will God forgive?"

What about the sins of adultery and murder? Can a murderer or adulterer ever find cleansing and closeness with God? Could Michael be restored to intimacy with Christ and usefulness in pastoral ministry?

King David, the towering military, administrative, and musical genius of the Old Testament, soared like a shooting star from the obscurity of the shepherd's field to the stardom of the palace. In one night, his blazing light of witness became a black hole of lust and then murder. Let's examine what his fall teaches us about the pull of lust and violence and about the restorative power of God's forgiveness. David was the "Sweet Singer of Israel." Did he ever sing freely again after the Bathsheba and Uriah affair?

The Anatomy of Adultery (2 Samuel 11:1-5)
The Midlife Time Out

> *In the spring, at the time when kings go off to war, David sent Joab out with the king's men and the whole Israelite army. They destroyed the Ammonites and besieged Rabbah. But David remained in Jerusalem. (2 Sam. 11:1)*

The primary responsibility of government is to protect the people under its care. In the ancient world, this responsibility fell on the shoulders of the king. He was the commander and chief of the military.

The fall rainy season and winter cold of Palestine made it impossible to move horses, chariots, and foot soldiers on to the field of battle. Thus, the ancient kings of the Near East called time-out in winter. Spring, however, blew the whistle for the resumption of hostilities. Ammon's declaration of war the previous year threatened Israel's security and David, God's ordained king, was responsible for defending the lives of the women and children of his nation. But this spring, David called a personal time out.

The forty-year-old giant killer, a veteran of campaigns against Philistines, Amalekites, Edomites, Moabites, and Arameans decided he deserved a break (2 Sam. 8). Others needed to gain experience in fighting the Lord's battles. David had reached the top, and from this vantage point, he found it easy to convince himself that he deserved a break. David experienced midlife crisis in 1000 B.C.

Midlife crises simply signal another major transition period in our lives. Whenever we reach some goal of success in business, education, or ministry and we begin to wonder if it was worth the effort if it gave us the thrill and sense of meaning we dreamed it would we become vulnerable to a period of crisis. This can become the first step in the anatomy of an affair.

I am not speaking about the legitimate need to come apart and rest. My father wisely taught me that if I don't take some time to rejuvenate, I will simply come apart. We live in enemy territory with a man-eating lion on the prowl seeking to devour us. Because Peter knew firsthand the peril of taking a nap on a spiritual battlefield, he urges us to *"be self-controlled and alert. Your enemy the devil prowls around like a roaring lion looking for someone to devour"* (1 Pet. 5:8).

For me as a pastor, this happens after I have done the ego fulfilling things, like building a beautiful church, speaking at prestigious conferences, or getting a book published that I begin to think that I deserve a vacation from the spiritual warfare, perhaps a little distance from my Savior. When our drive is fueled by ego, success creates a boring vacuum that Satan delights to fill. David forgot this fundamental principle of spiritual warfare and left his flank exposed.

The Visual Dream Woman

One evening David got up from his bed and walked around on the roof of the palace. From the roof he saw a woman bathing. The woman was very beautiful, and David sent someone to find out about her. The man said, "Isn't this Bathsheba, the daughter of Eliam and the wife of Uriah the Hittite?" (2 Sam. 11:2-3)

When we take an illegitimate break, we sleep when we should be awake, and we are awake when we should be asleep. Our schedules get reversed. David was no exception. In the evening, when working people were going to bed, David was just getting up from an afternoon

109

nap. He went on top of his flat-roofed house to chase away the sleep, and there he saw the voluptuous Bathsheba for the first time.

That Bathsheba's naked beauty caught David's attention was not sinful; it was normal. All David needed to do then was look away and say, "Thank you, Lord, for my sister Israelite's beauty. With her looks, I am sure that some gentleman has committed his life to her. Help them to enjoy one another. Thank you for the wife you have given me." If David would have talked to God like this, Bathsheba would not have become illicitly pregnant, and Uriah would have lived a lot longer.

Sexual lust is not defeated by labeling the beauty of the naked body as sinful. The sin is not in the nakedness. We have seen how the Song of Songs pictures a wife dancing naked before her husband (6:13-7:8). Sin lies in the intention of the human heart to steal something for its own that God has not given it.

Also, the initial invasion of a lustful thought into our mind is not sin. We break God's commands when this thought is allowed to give birth to the willful desire to fulfill the act of fornication or adultery. We are not defeated simply because the line of a woman's body captures our eyes and generates erotic thoughts.

Many years ago, a student at Dallas Seminary was chauffeur for the school's president, Lewis Sperry Chafer. One day, the elderly seminary president could not help but notice that his driver was visibly depressed. "What's the matter, son? You look like you just flunked theology," quipped Chafer.

"I am going to have to leave seminary," the young man replied.

"What for?"

The student hesitated to answer. So Dr. Chafer waited. Finally, the fellow blurted out in a barely understandable confession, "My thought life ... a pretty girl walks by and ...sexual ideas immediately invade my mind. I can't control the instant reaction. How can I ever be a preacher with thoughts like that entering my head?"

Dr. Chafer said nothing for a moment, and then quietly broke the silence, "What are *we* going to do?"

Like Martin Luther, Dr. Chafer understood the difference between temptation and willfully conceived lust. Luther told his students, "You can't keep the birds from flying over your head, but you can keep them from making a nest in your hair." David forgot this distinction. Instead of turning his thoughts home to God's plan for sexual fulfillment, he turned his inquiry into an invitation to adultery. The lust in David's eyes craved fulfillment in the physical desires of his body (1 John 2:16). Satan pushed David to make his mental dream woman materialize in his bed even though she belonged to another man.

The Physical Act of Adultery

> David sent messengers to get her. She came to him, and he slept with her. (She had purified herself from her uncleanness.) Then she went back home. The woman had conceived and sent word to David, saying, "I am pregnant."
> (2 Sam. 11:4-5)

David ignored all the warning signs—all his servants knew she was Eliam's daughter and the wife of Uriah, one of David's mighty men (11:3). Adulterers ignore the connectedness of the object of their lust to parents and to spouse. They choose to forget God's command, "You shall not commit adultery" (Ex. 20:14). High on a drug-like passion they believe no one, not even God, will ever know.

David thought he could have the ultimate sexual high—a one-night stand with a mysterious beauty. They could have their moment of ecstasy. She could return home, and no one would ever know the difference. But sex is never safe when it is immoral.

Discreetly, the biblical narrator informs us that David and Bathsheba had relations at an extremely critical time. According to Leviticus 15 during a woman's menstrual period, she was ceremonially unclean for seven days. Her husband was not to have relations with her during this time. On the eighth day, she was to take a small sacrifice to the temple and then return to take a sacred bath. She then invited her husband back in bed with her. This practice is the opposite of the rhythm method of birth control and guaranteed much pleasure and fertility to Israelite couples.

A woman's erotic desires and pleasures peak about a week after the cessation of her period. Both husband and wife should enjoy this time to the maximum. Tragically, it is also a period of dangerous seduction when a woman's husband is on the road. Bathsheba came into David at a time of critical vulnerability and intense fertility.

Many of our young people do not know their times of increased vulnerability. Our teenage daughters need to be taught how God has designed them sexually. Both young men and women should be cautious during this critical period. An understanding of how God has designed us sexually will make us sensitive to times of increased vulnerability.

Bathsheba was vulnerable. Her husband had been away at war for several weeks. She had just completed her time of uncleanness, had taken her ritual bath, and now she faced the usual time of marital fulfillment. Her meeting with David was like the union of fire and high octane gasoline.

David and Bathsheba also expose the fallacy of believing that only "bad" people get in trouble. David was the writer of inspired sacred Scripture. Bathsheba meticulously fulfilled the Levitical rules and regulations. Being a church leader or engaging in spiritual activities does not immunize us from the moral diseases of adultery or fornication. Often religious instructors angrily condemn the way kids dress and warn against the dangers of holding hands, when the issue is how to keep from having intercourse after school when both their parents are still at work. God's Word is not naive, and it is time we allowed God's inspired instruction to teach us and our children about our sexual vulnerabilities. Good religious people, like David and Bathsheba, entertain lust in their hearts. The wise person honestly faces his or her potential for immorality.

Bathsheba returned to her home. David believed the story would end in the thrill of a glorious one night stand. Everyone knows nothing happens when you do it only once. Often it does not, but illicit sex is like playing Russian roulette. Teenagers and adults today feel prepared with their contraceptives and condoms. Few face the truth that in the moment of passion, precautions are often forgotten. This explains the hideous fact that abortion has become a major solution to unwanted pregnancies. Bathsheba's note, "I am pregnant!" jolted David from fantasy island. What does a bright young king do with a note like that? Like every child caught with his hand in the cookie jar, he seeks to conceal his sin. A genius comes up with an ingenious cover-up.

The Anatomy of a Murder (2 Samuel 11:6-27)

Operation Cover-Up #1: *Conceal the Identity of the Real Father*

> *So David sent this word to Joab: "Send me Uriah the Hittite." And Joab sent him to David. When Uriah came to him, David asked him how Joab was, how the soldiers were and how the war was going. Then David said to Uriah, "Go down to your house and wash your feet." So Uriah left the palace, and a gift from the king was sent after him. But Uriah slept at the entrance to the palace with all his master's servants and did not go down to his house. When David was told, "Uriah did not go home," he asked him, "Haven't you just come from a distance? Why didn't you go home?"*
>
> *Uriah said to David, "The ark and Israel and Judah are staying in tents, and my master Joab and my lord's men are camped in the open fields. How could I go to my house to eat and drink and lie with my wife? As surely as you live, I will not do such a thing!"* (2 Sam. 11:6-11)

Like viewers watching the victim of a soap opera, all of David's servants know of his affair with Bathsheba and the reason for Uriah's sudden summons from the battlefield. King David believes he is covering everything up, but he is the sop. What he did undercover was the gossip of flapping lips within the palace. His plan to get Uriah to have intercourse with Bathsheba so that he will believe David's baby is his own is foiled by Uriah's personal godliness.

He is a foreign proselyte and a devout worshiper who obeys God's commands for holy war. Unlike his king, he obeyed God's ban against

113

intercourse during a sacred campaign. The Hebrew storyteller skillfully contrasts the king, who has no qualms about going to bed with another man's wife, with the foreigner, Uriah, who maintains the sacred vows in honor of God and nation.

Adultery in the life of one of God's children always causes him to act like the Devil's child. Denial will blind him to the open scandal of his sin, and his attempts to cover the affair will sink him deeper into deception. Uriah's consistent ethics caused David's operation cover-up #1 to fail miserably. But instead of honestly facing his sin and confessing it to God and to those involved, David's mind raced to the implementation of phase two.

Operation Cover-Up #2: Get the Husband Drunk So He Will Make Love To His Wife

David said to him, "Stay here one more day, and tomorrow I will send you back." So Uriah remained in Jerusalem that day and the next. At David's invitation, he ate and drank with him, and David made him drunk. But in the evening Uriah went out to sleep on his mat among his master's servants; he did not go home. (2 Sam. 11:12-13)

A few drinks can lower inhibitions; many can obliterate them. In the Ancient Near East when your monarch invited you for supper and poured you some wine, you drank. Israel's proverbial wisdom warned government leaders against the dangers of alcohol in the palace (Prov. 31:4), but the adulterous King David ignored common wisdom and decency. He poured the drinks for Uriah until his soldier became drunk. Once again David's plan displayed genius. The intoxicated husband would forget his religious scruples and make love to his wife. Sadly for David, the alcohol made Uriah feel like sleeping instead of making love. He stumbled to his bed among David's servants while Bathsheba continued to sleep alone.

The alcohol-sex connection should be well known to our children and to ourselves. Remember Noah, naked and drunk in his tent? How many young men and women have frivolously given away their virginity because their moral vision was clouded by too much alcohol? David tried to use this sex-alcohol connection to hide his own immorality, but again he failed. If he had only stopped covering and openly exposed his sin at this point, two innocent lives would not have been sacrificed.

Operation Cover-Up #3: Murder the Husband

In the morning David wrote a letter to Joab and sent it with Uriah. In it he wrote, "Put Uriah in the front line where the fighting is fiercest. Then withdraw from him so he will be struck down and die." So while Joab had the city under siege, he put Uriah at a place where he knew the strongest defenders were. When the men of the city came out and fought against Joab, some of the men in David's army fell; moreover, Uriah the Hittite was dead. (2 Sam. 11:14-17)

Few recognize that the passion that seizes a man and leads him to steal another man's wife is bound up with the cruelty that plots the murder of a human life. Cover-up #3 gets dirty as David realizes Uriah will not break his holy war vow and have relations with his wife. Uriah must be exterminated. David knows Uriah is so dependable he can be trusted to carry a letter containing his own death warrant without discovering its contents. David's letter was a premeditated plan, guaranteed to slay one of Israel's bravest soldiers.

With dramatic control David fakes surprise at the fatal results of the battle. He responds to Joab's report by saying,

Don't let this upset you; the sword devours one as well as another. Press the attack against the city and destroy it. (2 Sam. 11:25)

David had the audacity to blame Uriah's death on the fates of war. And Joab, his general, would manipulate him for the rest of his life because of his duplicity in this affair. David would never be able to take a stand against his violent bloodshed. David's cover-up tangled him in the manipulation and fear of another's murder.

Bathsheba publicly mourned for her husband. When this time period ended, David acted the gallant hero and comforted the grieving widow by making her his queen. She then gave birth to their son, and everyone lived happily ever after. David wanted the drama to end here, but he forgot the true director of history.

David's servants, Joab, Joab's aid, and probably all of Israel knew of his adultery. But the immoral king believed, as almost all adulterers do, that his sin was strictly private. David forgot about the omnipresent eyes of the ultimate King: *"But the thing David had done displeased the Lord"* (2 Sam. 11:27).

Television shows, movies, and novels often contradict the real consequences of adultery. Breathtaking Bathshebas go to be with handsome Davids repeatedly. These young professionals have risen above common morals. They do not need to marry or keep sacred vows. But the sovereign divine King still warns us that murder and adultery displease Him. They anger Him because they destroy human life and the sacred purpose for making love. Immorality never builds stable homes in which children feel secure. It leads to lies, deception, and violence. The guilt destroys a man and woman physically, emotionally, and spiritually. David's story cries out for us to obey the seventh commandment. But does God banish the murderous adulterer? Can God put Humpty Dumpty together again?

Chapter 10

Exposing a Cover-Up

How can we reach someone enslaved in the clutches of adultery or other forms of sexual immorality? Should we allow them to face the consequences of their behavior? When should we confront them concerning their sin? How can we get beneath their defensiveness and help them face their problem instead of erecting a barrier between us?

In the last chapter, David dramatically illustrated the web of deceit and violence that the denial of sin generates. In 2 Samuel 12, Nathan the prophet teaches us about timing, sensitivity to the Lord, and the power of a story to expose a cover-up. The prophet teaches us how to rescue an individual ensnared in sin.

Timing

David's sin disgusted the Lord, but for almost a year God permitted David to sink in the consequences of his deception. Psalm 32 presents David's personal testimony of his debilitating guilt—the aches and pains, the weakness, the depression. God waited until Bathsheba's pregnancy reached full term, and the baby was born before He sent His servant to David.

Love is patient, and if we are to be effective in healing the broken lives of immoral people, we need to learn to give the Spirit of God time to soften the opposition. We must aim to strike a delicate balance between two extremes: being too passive, allowing sin to fester into a serious life-threatening disease; and being too aggressive, causing the rebellious spirit to harden into granite.

The fact that Nathan did not go immediately to David as soon as the adultery and murder took place should caution us about trying to get involved immediately when sin grips the life of another. Sometimes God can restore an individual without the embarrassment of our intervention. Lives, like broken bones, need to be handled with gentleness. It takes time to be sure of the facts, to give God opportunity to work, and to examine our own motives for confrontation. Galatians 6:1 assigns the task of restoring those who have fallen to individuals who are controlled by the Holy Spirit. The Spirit is sensitive to timing.

God's Guidance

"The LORD sent Nathan to David." (2 Sam. 12:1)

Nathan's prophetic gift gave him direct access to the voice of God. In the Old Testament, God spoke to His prophets through a direct audible voice, sometimes in dreams or visions. Nathan was certain God sent him to intervene in David's life. How can we know when the Lord is sending us? Direct involvement makes this decision easier.

When someone's sin directly wounds us we are to go privately to them, reveal their fault, and seek to restore the relationship (Matt. 18:15). For example, suppose you are eating out with another couple. Since they called and initiated the invitation, you conclude that the bill will be handled separately or picked up by the other couple. Instead, at the conclusion of the meal, the nonverbal sign of moving the check close to your plate and your friend's casual remark, "Please, let me get the tip," gives the clear message that you are to pay the bill. This manipulation of your generosity makes you righteously angry and harms your closeness with this couple. In these cases, we know the facts, since we were involved, and a quick, direct conversation between friends can be used to either clarify a misunderstanding or to teach the biblical principle of not freeloading meals off another (2 Thess. 3:7-8). The offense can be removed and the friendship strengthened.

When a believer becomes engaged in unrepentant sin, his lifestyle is openly exposed to others, and the individual refuses to turn away from his destructive behavior, 1 Corinthians 5 exhorts fellow believers to put him out of their fellowship. Habitual wickedness—immorality, greed, idolatry, slander, drunkenness, and swindling—should not be tolerated in the lives of those who call themselves believers in Christ (1 Cor. 5:11). We are to forgive the sinner who asks forgiveness seventy

118

times seven, but we must love one another enough not to allow blatant rebellion against God to go unchallenged.

A father can love his nineteen-year-old son but he can not allow this son to mock his authority by repeatedly coming home drunk, sleeping with women in the house, and stealing money from his wallet. The son must be ordered to leave the home. The story of the Prodigal illustrates how the Heavenly Daddy handles this crisis (Luke 15). Perhaps when the son faces the full impact of his behavior, he will turn away from his self-destructive foolishness. If this lesson is learned, the child is to be invited home to a warm reception. The church family, likewise, is to restore the forgiven son to full participation with the worshiping community (2 Cor. 2:5-8).

The matter of restoration becomes difficult when you are not directly influenced by another's sin and when they skillfully cover it, acting as though nothing is wrong. Immorality often falls into this category. It can be extremely difficult to prove. In these cases, the force of circumstantial evidence and sensitivity to the Holy Spirit's internal promptings must guide us.

Nathan was a prophet who received direct revelations from God. But the Hebrew narrator of 2 Samuel makes it clear that an inspired message is not always necessary to begin to question the spiritual health of another. The murmurings from David's household concerning an affair, the tragic death of Bathsheba's husband, the hurry-up wedding, the baby born full size before full term, David's physical and emotional deterioration—the evidence was strong and clear. Circumstantial evidence does not prove a person's guilt, but a pile of hints should demand a confrontation.

Like Nathan, we need to learn to smell the smoke so we can go and put out the fire. Those who listen daily to the voice of God in the Scripture and talk to Him in prayer are the most sensitive to the quiet promptings of the Holy Spirit, who points to people in need of direction and presses the need to take the initiative to restore a wandering brother or sister to Christ.

Storytelling: The Hard-Heart Softener

Nathan came to David with a story, not a sermon. We need to learn the power of the "Once upon a time" to move gently beneath the defenses and penetrate to the heart of a prodigal's soul. Nathan knew the way to bring conviction and repentance to a hostile soul. He began,

> *"There were two men in a certain town, one rich and the other poor. The rich man had a very large number of sheep and cattle, but the poor man had nothing except one little ewe lamb he had bought. He raised it, and it grew up with him and his children. It shared his food, drank from his cup and even slept in his arms. It was like a daughter to him.*
>
> *Now a traveler came to the rich man, but the rich man refrained from taking one of his own sheep or cattle to prepare a meal for the traveler who had come to him. Instead, he took the ewe lamb that belonged to the poor man and prepared it for the one who had come to him."*
>
> *David burned with anger against the man and said to Nathan, "As surely as the Lord lives, the man who has done this deserves to die. He must pay for that lamb four times over, because he did such a thing and had no pity."*
>
> *Then Nathan said to David, "You are the man!"*
> (2 Sam. 12:1-7)

As in our modern world where some animal rights activists cry over the death of dolphins but shed no tears over millions of murdered babies, David could cry over the death of a pet lamb but suppress his guilt over the spilled blood of a man. Nathan's story, however, graphically displayed the true nature of adultery. It was senseless robbery. Ironically, he stole not to gain what he did not have but what he already possessed in abundance (2 Sam. 12:8).

How many husbands try to steal pleasure from a forbidden woman when all the enjoyment they could ever want is available in the partner of their youth who slept next to them for years? Satan calls adultery a destined affair of love. God still calls it stealing. It can unleash the fury of violence. Whenever God's principles are despised by ignorance or lethargy, it leads to death. David tried to tell Joab the loss of soldiers was not evil, but this human rationalization could not change God's verdict—murder and adultery were crimes (2 Sam. 12:9).

As certainly as like gives birth to like, sin releases a flow of circumstances only the grace of God can enable one to endure. Because of David's bloodshed, his reign would be marred with murder. Because of his immorality, sex scandals would plague his family. Satan's deceit and violence would be allowed to take its toll. In a society of no-fault, no-consequence sin the judgment word God spoke against David needs to be heard again (2 Sam. 12:9-12). David and his family are left scarred for the rest of their lives. Agonizing tears are spilled over the legacy of murderous violence and immorality that resides in his sons. But is this the end of David's story; does the flaming meteor fizzle in a black hole of death?

Nathan assured David that he would not die. And in the midst of sin's consequences, the forgiven David sang some of his greatest songs. For the meaning of life in the Bible is not cold obedience to a set of moral laws but passionate devotion to the Savior because of His amazing, forgiving grace. Nathan's "You are the man!" was not God's last word to King David or to those today who commit the robbery and violence of immorality.

Chapter 11

Forgiveness—The Song of Renewal

The spring pastor's retreat provided three days of escape and recuperation from the grind of hospital visits, counseling hours, and sermon preparation. Usually George Lewis hungered for this time with the other pastors in his denomination but this April, driving up the Interstate, he thoughtfully sorted through a pile of reasons to turn around and go home. His son's immorality made him dread the reunion with his associates. He remembered last year's retreat—the usual questions around the meal table. "How's Michael's church going? Didn't he start a work out of a Bible study a few years ago[1]?"

His father's heart swelled with pride as he responded to these repeated questions. He savored the pats on the back as Michael's ministry success advertised his effectiveness as a father, the "good home manager" of 1 Timothy 3. This year, he dreaded the questions and the silence. Those who knew about Michael's fall would feel sorry for him. Like dealing with someone who has just experienced a death in the family, they would refrain from bringing up the hurt. But George needed to talk, to open up about how to keep pastoring when one of your children fails morally. He needed to discuss and pray with his brothers in the ministry to learn how he should counsel Michael. He needed the answers to the tough questions: How can a pastor find forgiveness when he has committed adultery with his secretary? Has he forever forfeited the right to be honored as a leader in Christ's family? Must he sell insurance, go into secular teaching, or administrate a retirement retreat instead of using his gift of teaching to build up the church? Does immorality spell death to one's ministry?

George arrived at his exit and turned into the camp entrance about five o'clock. He would barely have time to throw his suitcase in his room and make it to supper and the evening meeting. This year's speaker raised curiosity. Instead of the usual avant-garde, big suburban pastor with his latest techniques for management and growth, Lewis Turnbull brought to the group his twenty-five years of faithful teaching, visiting, and shepherding experience in a rural Kansas community. "At least," George thought, "this guy ought to identify with the kinds of problems the average pastor faces." The seven o'clock meeting gave him a chance to find out.

After the usual, "we're thrilled to have you" introduction and the recitation of his pedigree, Turnbull began,

"Men, our society craves strong moral leadership. Though sexual and monetary cheating is epidemic, the majority vote only for leaders whose backgrounds are free of scandalous pot, sex, or alcohol abuse detectable by the media. Faced with this duality—a moral cesspool, yet an intense desire for consistent ethics—the church is in danger of turning the biblical message into a sermon on consistent obedience to moral law instead of the joyful shout of forgiveness found in moments of grace. Twenty-five years of working with people has convinced me that the Bible isn't lying when it says, 'There is none righteous, no not one.' There is no sinless individual, no perfect family. Everyone has their dark side that, if exposed, would require the eternal death penalty. This Romans 1-3 message needs to be recaptured in our churches. We need to be honest about the deadliness of our moral tumors so that we can rejoice in the power of the divine radiation to destroy them.

"The church vacillates between a legal rigidity that rejects the fallen and joins the secular world in its hardened unforgiveness against the exposed sinner, and a cheap grace that cuddles the habitual sin addict by accepting his tears of remorse as genuine repentance. We hedge about the validity of true guilt. We are confused about the nature of true confession.

"Genuine guilt, not AIDS, is the worst infection threatening humankind. It eats away our souls. Drink cannot wash away dirty consciences. Drugs fail to dull the senses long enough to escape sin's condemnation. Psychoanalysis exposes guilt's sources and calms its effects when no real wrong has occurred. But how do we get rid of the burden when the naked truth is that we did something authentically and horribly? How do you spell relief when promises have been shattered, purity has been soiled, lives have been cruelly butchered? We must know how to find forgiveness for real sin producing real guilt in our consciences. We must allow God to teach us the nature of true confession and how to treat the fallen when God declares them cleansed.

"Psalm 51 lets us inside the mind of the adulterous murderer King David at the strategic moment—the instant of destiny—when Nathan put his finger on his sin and said, 'You are the man!' Observe the superscription to the Psalm. David's heart response exposes the difference between repentance and remorse. His conclusion to his confession answers the questions, 'How should we treat the forgiven?' 'Who is qualified to teach—who has something to teach—in the household of God?' The heavenly grading of this Old Testament saint in an age of law proclaims mercy and forgiveness to New Testament saints in the age of grace. David's fall and restoration puts its finger on the true essence of human life from a divine perspective."

> **Genuine guilt, not AIDS, is the worst infection threatening humankind. It eats away our souls. Drink cannot wash away dirty consciences.**

As an older pastor, George did not usually take notes from a speaker. But during this introduction, he found himself reaching in his shirt pocket and taking out a scratch pad. Because of his own son's immorality, he needed this message from Psalm 51, not for a Sunday morning message for his congregation but for his own existence. The following verses show the essence of the notations he made.

Grace Not Merit—The Basis of Forgiveness

Have mercy on me, O God, according to your unfailing love;
according to your great compassion blot out my transgressions.

Wash away all my iniquity and cleanse me from my sin.
(Ps. 51:1-2)

David's initial appeal goes to the core of the nature of sin, of God, and of forgiveness. When he received word of Uriah's death, he lamely tried to convince himself and Joab that nothing "evil" had occurred (2 Sam. 11:25). After Nathan's confrontation, David agreed with God's assessment of his adultery and murder. It was rebellion and perversion—a treacherous fracturing of his intimate covenant relationship with God.

As long as we treat God's commands against fornication and adultery like the 65 mph speed limit we exceed in the absence of a police officer with his radar gun, we fail to discern the heart of sin. Sin is more than a failure to comply with arbitrary rules. It shatters intimacy. Like a son punching his dad in the face, it arrogantly mocks the Heavenly Father's authority and love. No good works can undo this breach of relationship. This explains why David cried for "mercy," not another chance.

David based his appeal for forgiveness not in promises to do better but in God's incredible gracious loyalty to His covenant with him (2 Sam. 7). With no defense, he cried out, "God show mercy to the guilty." He admitted his failure to live up to the mutual obligations flowing from his unity with God, but he remembered God's heart for humankind. Beginning in the Garden, man consistently fails to live up to his side of his obligations toward his Creator, but God overwhelms these failures with His undeserved promises of blessing. Man's sin cannot quench God's desire to love.

This divine loyalty is more tenacious than the compassion a mother feels for the child she carried in her womb. Forgiveness flows from this womb-like tenderness God feels for His babies. Human parents sometimes quit on their children, but the Ultimate Father's heart stirs within to restore His child. When grievous sin stains our heart, Satan attacks with his potent lie—"God has given up on you—the relationship is over. Why return to a Father who has disowned you?" True confession breaks through this deception and remembers God's unchanging mercy, loyalty, and compassion. When God's rebellious children cry out for mercy, He always listens. He gives far more than a spot cleaning. He bleaches out every stain.

Forgiveness for us is often a shallow, "It's no big deal. Forget it," when internally we are thinking, "I'll never trust you again as a friend." God's forgiveness is more than a passive, "It's okay." He thoroughly scrubs away the moral filth.

He blots out the record of sin in His heavenly court records. He heals the moral infection within.

> Christ's character makes His forgiveness reliable. His cross makes it just, and His present resurrected position at the seat of authority over the universe guarantees that no sin escapes His right to forgive.

I remember as a kid in grammar school, before the days of Powerpoint and Photoship, when blackboards were the common teaching tool. My teacher would write, erase, and then write again where she had erased. By the end of the day the board was totally illegible. The residue of chalk left by the eraser, combined with the mess of new writing, turned spelling words into an impenetrable code—a mass of white chalk marks.

After the last bell, the janitor arrived with his pail of water and a cloth. Dampening the cloth in his bucket he then wiped the slate clean. Unlike the previous felt eraser technique, the wet cloth thoroughly obliterated the scratching of the day. Divine forgiveness is no surface eraser job. He wipes the records clean. David appeals for this thorough cleansing in Psalm 51:1-2 before the divine Supreme Court Justice. What attitudes open the door to His merciful forgiveness?

Repentance Not Remorse—True Confession

The unrepentant sinner denies guilt, refuses to face the true offended party, schemes to avert punishment, and fails to face the deep evil that has taken root. Psalm 51:3-6 reveals how true confession repudiates all of these defense mechanisms and fosters honesty before God.

The Denial of Denial

I know my transgressions, and my sin is always before me.
(Ps. 51:3)

Unrepentant sinners become unconscious of their guilt. This refusal to admit what in fact has happened is one of the most bizarre characteristics of sexual sin. During the year of David's cover-up, he described the intense physical and emotional deterioration he experienced (Ps. 32). If David had lived this experience in our day, I can picture him making frequent visits to the hospital for medical tests and to a psychologist to determine the underlying cause for this disturbance in his internal equilibrium. Yet in this case, the root problem was not physical or psychological. God's moral standards had been violated. Not until Nathan put his finger in David's face did he become aware that the true cause of his physical and emotional collapse was his spiritual treachery. Deception is intrinsic to sinfulness. The truth must penetrate this amoral haze for genuine repentance to occur.

Sexual immorality loves to pose as a beautiful "spiritual affection"—the promise of unfulfilled dreams. The battle between the ecstasy of the personal oneness and the painfulness of facing the real life complications arising from this forbidden love often drive the mind to pretend that no wrong has occurred.

Susan began to listen to these false promises of illicit love at a Christian camp and ended up denying the reality that she was breaking the seventh commandment. She could not believe her unsaved husband actually gave her permission to accompany her church youth group when they needed another adult sponsor. He always responded coldly to anything to do with church, but, this time he said, "Take the kids to your mom's, put some meals for me in the freezer, and go ahead and leave me for a week."

Susan found it hard to believe he let her go, but the rickety church bus jostled home the reality. The first night in the chow line she noticed Skip. He was laughing with some friends, but his eyes spoke of sadness. While she ate the burned chicken, her ears picked up on the conversation at the next table when one of the counselors mentioned that Skip had lost his wife to cancer a year earlier. After Skip and Susan were given the responsibility for the afternoon recreation period, she found herself looking forward to the close planning sessions with him each morning.

Skip proved to be deeply concerned about spiritual things, gentle and skillful at putting into words how he felt. Susan prayed with him after their planning each morning and cherished the oneness of being used together to help the teenagers that week learn about Jesus Christ. Their planning sessions left recreation far behind as Skip shared his numbness, loneliness, and anger in the face of the loss of his loved one. Susan shared the frustration of living with a husband who didn't have a spiritual bone in his body. Her difficulty in saying goodbye on Saturday morning surprised her.

The intense spiritual high of the week at camp soon burned out in the boring grind of normal family responsibilities. Her husband continued to sleep till 10:00 on Sunday morning and then fish till sundown. Susan hated sitting husbandless in church. She was uneasy about the persistent intrusion of Skip into her thoughts. She quickly repressed her intense yearnings for time with him. At least her increased involvement with the youth group kept her mind occupied and made her feel worthwhile and alive.

The invitation from her pastor to attend a weekend fall seminar dealing with youth ministries looked like the perfect opportunity to increase her effectiveness as a teacher. The flight to Chicago, shuttle ride to the hotel, and mingling with the sophisticated business people in the plush hotel lobby made her feel far removed from home.

She could not believe her eyes when she walked into the meeting room that night, and Skip was sitting about a third of the way up the aisle. She tried in vain to pay attention to the introductory lecture. She could hardly wait until its conclusion.

They went together to a nearby restaurant and talked till 1:00 a.m. The elevator and the hall were empty and silent as Skip accompanied Susan to her room. It was too easy for him to open her door, walk inside, and gather her in his arms. A widower's loneliness and a housewife's hunger pains for love fueled their sexual desires that night. When Skip checked the hall at four o'clock it was still empty, and he returned to his room. The threat of discovery only heightened the intensity of their affair over the next six months. Ingenious plots enabled them to get together frequently.

When home Susan poured herself into being a good mother and cooking fantastic meals. She was amazed at her newly discovered patience with her husband. With her family the affair evaporated into fantasy, but the dream switched to white hot reality when she could get away. She lived for those secret moments alone with Skip.

The secular world proclaims it is an adult's right to satisfy these unfulfilled dreams and drives. The Christian world denies the power of this undertow toward illicit love. Believers doubt that denial can cause people to split their lives so drastically. But until Susan and Skip honestly face that "it *can* be wrong when it feels so right," they will remain estranged from the only true lover of their souls. They must join David and say, "I know my transgressions, and my sin is always before me." The loving Father has not changed His mind—adultery is still wrong. We all must reckon with our rejection of God's absolutes.

The Real Offended Party

Against you, you only, have I sinned and done what is evil in your sight. (Ps. 51:4)

Our sins harm our lives and others, but the true pain is in God's heart. By definition, sin is treachery against a covenant relationship of love with Him and rebellion against His revealed will; thus, though Uriah died, and Susan's husband and family were betrayed, God was the ultimate person abused. Remorse wails over the harm brought upon others and whimpers in low self-esteem, but true confession gets face-to-face with God and starts telling the truth.

The Acceptance of the Justice of Punishment

You are proved right when you speak and justified when you judge. (Ps. 51:4)

130

Barton's court case would begin at nine o'clock the next morning. He sat in his pastor's study. It was difficult to understand his question through the tears.

"Would you be willing to testify on my behalf tomorrow?"

John hesitated to respond.

"Over the last several weeks you have admitted to me that you repeatedly committed incest against your daughter. As a witness in court, I would take an oath promising to tell the truth. As your counselor, I want to help you, but in light of your confessions do you honestly want me for a character witness in courts?"

Barton glanced up at John. "Then how do you think I should defend myself before the judge?"

"I think you should plead guilty. Tell your lawyer to drop the defense and cast yourself upon the mercy of the court. Accept the truth! You deserve whatever sentence the law demands for this crime. Free your daughter from the embarrassment of rehearsing the painful details in another public hearing. If I were your judge in this case, your willingness to accept the justice of my sentence would demonstrate a genuine desire to turn away from your criminal acts. Barton, are you pleading innocent or guilty?"

John prayed Barton's tears were signs of change, not manipulation. Sadly, his response exposed the continued self-centeredness of his addiction.

"But that will mean state prison. The inmates will kill me if they find out my crime. My lawyer says we have a chance of creating some doubt about the extent of the sexual contact."

The difference between remorse and repentance is difficult to discern. Barton's rejection of the judge's right to punish him and his continued self-defense is a strong indication that he has not escaped from the cycle of addiction that causes him to commit the unmentionable perversion of a father's relationship with his daughter.

In contrast, David demonstrated true repentance, a 180 degree turn in his heart, when he acknowledged God's rightness in judging him (Ps. 51:4). When Nathan pronounced the sentence of a lifetime of war, the murderous immoral conflict in his family, and the death of his child, David did not protest. He simply replied, *"I have sinned!"* (2 Sam. 12:7-14). Years later, when Shimei hurled curses and stones at him as he fled Jerusalem to escape the coup attempt by his son, Absalom, David still did not protest God's right to punish him for his sin; yet he continued to count on the power of God's mercy to turn the cursing into blessing (2 Sam. 16:5-14). With the thief on the cross, true confession admits, *"We are punished justly, for we are getting what our deeds deserve"* (Luke 23:41). When we reject denial, face the true offended party, and acknowledge God's right to punish us, we penetrate to the source of our immorality.

The Root of Immorality

> *Surely I was sinful at birth, sinful from the time my mother conceived me.*
> *Surely you desire truth in the inner parts; you teach me wisdom in the inmost place.* (Ps. 51:5-6)

False confession blames circumstances, the environment, society, or companions for its misdeeds. True confession accepts the divine diagnosis that we have inherited a humanly incurable, fatal, moral disease. David is not accusing his mother of conceiving him in an illicit relationship or saying that the enflamed passion of his parents' intercourse polluted him in some way. He simply acknowledges that sin is not an external problem controllable by self-discipline or a change in environment. Evil permeates the internal lining of the human personality from birth. Therefore, external solutions through legislation or religious rituals will never purify our putrid ethics. Jesus confirmed David's analysis—evil is centered at the core of the human heart (Mark 7:21-23; cf. Rom. 5:12). True confession honestly faces this internal root of evil.

God, however, has not left the human heart insulated from the voice of truth. Deep within, our consciences police our actions and condemn us when we fail to do what we believe is right. God seeks to defeat the internal deception and help us face the truth about how to live skillfully. God inscribed these principles not only on stone tablets for Moses but also in the fleshly tablets of our hearts (Rom. 2:15).

True confession honestly faces the intrinsic deception and evil deep in the human personality, and begins to listen to God's internal witness. If we keep listening, He will disclose to us the cure for genuine guilt.

Deliverance not Probation—The Assurance of Forgiveness

The Sacrificial Blood

> *Cleanse me with hyssop and I will be clean; wash me, and I will be whiter than snow... .*
> *Save me from bloodguilt, O God... .*
> *You do not delight in sacrifice, or I would bring it;*
> *you do not take pleasure in burnt offerings.*
> *The sacrifices of God are a broken spirit; a broken and contrite heart, O God, you will not despise.*
> (Ps. 51:7, 14, 16-17)

In Scripture, the stains of objective guilt can only be washed away by a literal blood sacrifice. Modern sensibilities scorn what is considered a primitive ceremony; satanic occultism creates a perverted fascination with bloody rituals; but only when we understand the meaning of sacrifice in the Old Testament and its fulfillment in the New do we realize the seriousness of our moral offenses and the cost of our forgiveness.

Hyssop was a plant, possibly marjoram or thyme, whose hairy stems when bunched together made an effective sprinkling apparatus. Thus, hyssop could be dipped in the blood of the sacrificed lamb and applied to the lintel and doorposts of the Israelite home in the Passover ritual (Ex. 12:22). When a virulent disease was cured, the priest declared the patient clean and healthy by sprinkling him or her with the blood of a sacrifice (Lev. 14:4, 6). David remembered these ceremonies but knew no ritual could cancel the penalty for adultery and murder. For these capital offenses, death was the sentence. Accepting the justice of this sentence, David cried out for mercy. He asked God to be his priest and sprinkle him with the blood that would declare him clean.

Not until John the Baptist identified Jesus as God's Lamb do we discern that He is the blood into which God dipped His hyssop branch to turn David's scarlet sins into the whiteness of new fallen snow. The religious rituals of the Old Testament sacrificial system never magically removed guilt. This explains David's repudiation of a ritual cult devoid of the humility and brokenness that alone touched God's compassion (Ps. 51:16). The animal sacrifices only acted as a powerful object lesson pointing forward to the ultimate offering for sin.

The New Testament writer of Hebrews explains for us how Christ set aside the animal sacrifices of the Old Testament with His once-for-all offering on Calvary (Heb. 10:8-10). The just payment for sin is death, and Christ's death forever paid this price.

When immoral people become conscious of their sin, Satan loves to condemn. When their heart breaks over the seriousness of their crime, he presents self-destruction as the payment they should make for their guilt. This blatant heinous lie comes from the pit of hell. Jesus Christ already died. There is no need for anyone to attempt to pay for his or her sin with suicide. For us to choose to reject Christ's gift is the epitome of conceit and deception. If the blood stains on David's hands could be cleaned by Christ's sacrifice, then nothing we have done is unforgivable. *"The blood of Jesus, his Son, purifies us from all sin"* (1 John 1:7b).

The Restored Joy of Salvation

Let me hear joy and gladness; let the bones you have crushed rejoice.

Hide your face from my sins and blot out all my iniquity.

Create in me a pure heart, O God, and renew a steadfast spirit within me.

Do not cast me from your presence or take your Holy Spirit from me.

Restore to me the joy of your salvation and grant me a willing spirit, to sustain me. (Ps. 51:8-12, 15)

True guilt steals our physical health and spiritual spontaneity. The clouds of alienation block the radiance of God's love. Our hearts harden in apathy, resistant to worship. The acceptance of God's forgiveness cures this heart condition. He restores physical vitality, clears our conscience, and gives us the willingness to praise Him again. He melts our cold, unfeeling heartlessness with the warmth of His Holy Spirit's control in our life.

Under the Old Covenant, the Spirit's residence in the human heart could be intermittent and temporary. Priests, prophets, and kings experienced His anointing at strategic moments for special divine purposes but could not depend upon His lifelong residence in their lives. David had good reason to beg God not to remove His Spirit from his heart. King Saul, his predecessor, failed to confess with sincerity and truth. The divine Spirit did leave him, and an evil spirit of suspicion and violence filled the emptiness. Saul ended his life with suicide on a defeated battlefield (1 Sam. 16:14; 31:4).

But David's heart was different from Saul's. David was concerned about his intimacy with God, not his popularity with the people. Thus, God's Spirit never departed; it dwelled with David for a lifetime.

Pentecost opened the door for this Spirit to take up permanent residence, not only in the hearts of kings and prophets, but in all of us who depend upon Christ for eternal forgiveness. This Spirit residence is God's deposit guaranteeing our heavenly inheritance. For the Spirit to abandon us would be tantamount to God breaking His personal pledge (Eph. 1:13-14). This confidence of His presence must never make us insensitive to the harm of hardened sin in the believer's life.

Under the New Covenant, we can still hurt Him deeply. Our lies, bitterness, slander, and deliberate willfulness that harms others grieves Him and will bring Him to discipline us (Eph. 4:30). Arrogant commitment to sinful behavior and resistance to His discipline can quench His purifying fire in our lives (1 Thess. 5:19). The sustained failure to respond to His convicting work can place our physical life in jeopardy as we are excluded from fellowship with God's family and become exposed to Satan's murderous attempts on our lives (1 Cor. 5:4-5; 1 Pet. 5:8). Only true confession will turn us away from resistance to the Spirit and cause us to become pliable in His hands, submissive to His desire to create the character of Christ in us. The loudest shouts of praise and joy burst forth from the sinner who experiences Christ's forgiveness and a renewed sensitivity to the Holy Spirit. Christ's character makes His forgiveness reliable, His cross makes it just, and His present resurrected position at the seat of authority over the universe guarantees that no sin escapes His right to forgive (1 John 1:9-2:2).

When the Apostle Paul summarized God's evaluation of David's life 1000 years after his death, he said, *"I have found David son of Jesse a man after my own heart; he will do everything I want him to do"* (Acts 13:22; cf. 1 Kgs. 9:4). How could God eulogize an adulterous murderer with this glowing tribute? Because forgiveness wipes the record clean.

The sweet singer of Israel did sing again after his horrible failure in the Bathsheba-Uriah affair. Psalm 51 reveals that he did more than sing in the choir, he taught again in the pulpit.

George Lewis eagerly shared this message of hope with his son, Michael, when he returned from the retreat. When he came to the point about forgiveness, Michael stopped him, "Dad, I know the Lord has forgiven me. I know He walks with me through life again. My horror is not that God will reject me from intimacy but that He will place me on the shelf marked 'UNUSABLE.' The Holy Spirit still gives me insight into the Scriptures. I hunger to feed God's people with this truth. But my immorality has forever disqualified me from leadership. I can never be a 'one woman man' again."

His dad never looked up, he simply read on, *"Then I will teach transgressors your ways, and sinners will turn back to you"* (Ps. 51:13).

"Son, this confession and Psalm 32 are probably the most powerful lines of poetry King David ever wrote. God inspired him to write both Psalm 51 and 32 after his adulterous murder. The Bible teachers who picture David's life as a bell curve that reached its zenith at 1 Samuel 10 and from then on descended into fruitlessness legitimately express their anger at the horror of sexual sin in a saint. They focus on the consequences of David's sin but fail to discern the power of grace in these difficulties. God was not in the life of the insulting, unforgiving Shimei. God walked with David into exile and then brought him back home. David's last words could answer, 'Yes,' when asked, 'Is not my house right with God?' He went on to write,

> *Blessed is he whose transgressions are forgiven, whose sins are covered.*
> *Blessed is the man whose sin the LORD does not count against him, and in whose spirit is no deceit.* (Ps. 32:1-2)

"Michael, if I wrote one line of Psalm 51 or Psalm 32, how could anyone consider my human life to be a failure, my ministry to have ended? The church must remember— you must believe—that God's mercy blots out adultery and murder with Calvary and anoints the forgiven sinner to proclaim this grace again. If Jesus could anoint Peter, the denier, to be the first pastor-teacher in the church, I am confident He will again use the gift of teaching He has graciously given you to cause sinners to repent and return to Himself.

"With Shimei some will throw stones and curses, some churches and Christian organizations will disqualify you from leadership, the secular world will never understand grace, but the Head of the Body will skillfully use you in His time and place for a lifetime."

Sex sin can be forgiven, and the Savior can restore the song of pure, Christ-like love for fallen ministers like Michael, housewives like Susan, lonely men like Skip, people like Matt and Sandra, and maybe someone like you. Jesus the Messiah has slain the serpent. Let's allow Him to deliver us all from the clutches of satanic sexuality.

Chapter 12
Conclusion

We have discovered that sex really is like nitroglycerin—it can be used to soothe hearts in marriage or to blow lives to pieces in immorality. When enthroned as a goddess, Sex becomes demonic and deadly, leading to destruction in individuals, families, and society. We have exposed Satan as the force behind this devastation. Sex sin must not be labeled as simply a physical or psychological maladjustment. Vital spiritual issues are at stake, and God's archrival has turned human sexuality into a battlefield where he seeks to destroy the Creator's design for sexual love between a man and a woman. Satan hates sex in marriage for it is an object lesson illustrating the Trinity, a picture of Christ's love for His church, and a foretaste of eternal bliss. He hurls his darts against God's illustration by tempting men and women to give in to illicit passion outside the boundaries of marriage.

Jesus Christ is the promised Male Deliverer who has defeated Satan's kingdom and can enable us to recapture God's original purpose for human sexuality. Only the power of Christ's love can overcome the power of lust. He alone can give us the power to say no to immorality, and yes to purity.

Calvary reveals the ultimate expression of love, and Christ's resurrection gives us the strength to follow His actions of love presented in 1 Corinthians 13.

We have challenged singles to enter relationships with the opposite sex through the door of Christ-like love and not through the intoxicating power of sexual contact. We discovered the example of Jesus as a single man. He enjoyed warm friendships not only with men, but also with women. His morally pure "brother-sister" relationships provide a model to help modern singles develop companionships with members of the opposite sex based on friendship and respect rather than sex. Contrary to the teaching of the "old school," healthy friendships between the sexes do not encourage immorality but protect against it. Pure sexual love can then grow out of the fertile soil of these relationships.

Married sexual love is exclusive. Sex is to be preserved for the one person who makes a vow before God to stay with you for a lifetime. Certainly God did not blush when He inspired the poet of the Song of Songs to vividly portray the ecstasy of sex in marriage. God commands His married children to make love. He designed them to fit together for more than procreation. Their union brings together the three circles of love—unselfish giving, personal sharing, and pleasure-filled physical union—into a holy picture of the oneness of the Trinity and Christ's intimacy with the church. The depth of this sexual experience exceeds the shallow temporary thrills of Satan's counterfeit affairs.

In the final section, we discovered the joy of restoration with the good news that Jesus Christ is capable of giving even the adulterous, murderous Davids and Bathshebas of this world a new song. In their forgiveness, they can become some of the most powerful witnesses to the grace of the cross and the necessity of absolute moral purity.

Let's conclude our discussion of sex in biblical focus by returning to the survey of the younger generation we met at the beginning of this book. I am concerned about their sources for the facts of life. By far the most frequent source they cited as their inside track on sex was their peers. Twice as many said, "I learned about sex from my friends" than said, "I learned about sex from my parents." The school of experience and pornographic magazines also scored higher than the parents as sources of sex information. Dad and Mom came in at about the same level as TV, movies, and sex education classes.

In homes where parents did muster the courage to speak openly about this delicate subject, mom was twice as likely to talk about it as dad. One of the girls wrote, "My mother made me get dressed up in my new birthday dress, and then she sat me down and explained everything about the facts of life to me." Another wrote, "My mother and I have always had a very close relationship, so I have felt comfortable talking to her about any questions I have had about sex. I am proud to say that I am still a virgin and I am saving myself for that one and only guy in marriage. He's out there somewhere!" Bravo for moms like this!

Not all the dads remained silent in their easy chairs about the most dominant subject on children's minds. One of the teens wrote, "I first learned about sex when my father explained it to me at about 12. I really do appreciate it. He gave me a biblical background on sex. I think because of his love for me this is why I have not and never will experience sex until marriage."

The church came in dead last as a place where these kids learned about sexuality. When friends talk about it freely and pornographic magazines score higher than the church as a source of information, Christian leaders dare not remain silent. I am thankful for voices that are speaking out clearly and biblically on this issue. As church leaders and teachers, as parents (especially dads), and as mature adults we need to face our responsibility to tell the truth about sex to the next generation. We must get over our embarrassment by biblically accepting our personal sexuality. We must discern the Heavenly Father's beliefs and blueprint concerning sex, and then get in there and intensely compete with our children's peers and the media for the attention of our children concerning this pervasive and powerful subject. In Christ, we can together again discover the celebration of love without shame.

Works Cited

Andersen, Francis and David Freedman. *Hosea*. Anchor Yale Bible Commentaries. New Haven, CT: Yale University Press, 1996. Commentary.

Barth, Markus. "Ephesians: Introduction, Translation, and Commentary on Chapters 4-6," vol. 2, *The Anchor Bible*. Garden City, NY: Doubleday, 1981. Bible.

Brown, Francis, S. R. Driver, and Charles Briggs, eds. *A Hebrew and English Lexicon of the Old Testament with an Appendix Containing the Biblical Aramaic*. Oxford: Clarendon, 1907. Lexicon.

Cassuto, U. *A Commentary on the Book of Genesis*, Part One. Jerusalem: The Magnes Press, The Hebrew University, 1972. Book.

Craigie, P.C., and G.H. Wilson, "Religions of the Biblical World: Canaanite," *The International Standard Bible Encyclopedia*, vol. 4, edited by Geoffrey W. Bromiley and Roland K. Harrison. Grand Rapids, MI: William B. Eerdmans Publishing Company, 1988. Encyclopedia.

Encyclopedia Britannica, s.v. "Syrian and Palestinian Religions," vol. 17. Encyclopedia.

Oakes, Lucia and Gahlin. *Ancient Egypt*. Leicester: Hermes House, 2006. Book.

Peck, Scott. *People of the Lie: The Hope for Healing Human Evil*, 2 ed. New York: Touchstone, 1998. Book.

Ringgren, Helmer. *Religions of the Ancient Near East*. Louisville, KY: Westminster Press, 1973. Book.

Ross, Allen P. *The Bible Knowledge Commentary: Old Testament*, edited by John F. Walvoord, Roy B. Zuck. Wheaton, IL: Victory Books,1985. Commentary.

Sailhamer, John H. *The Expositor's Bible Commentary: Genesis, Exodus, Leviticus, Numbers*, edited by Frank E. Gaebelein. Grand Rapids, MI: Zondervan, 1990. Commentary.

Saint Augustine, *Imperfectum Opus contra Iulianum.II*, edited by Michaela Zelzer. Charlottesville, VA: Hoelder-Pichler-Tempsky, 1974. Book.

Scorcese, Martin. "The Last Temptation of Christ," 1998. Movie.

Shalit, Wendy. *A Return to Modesty:Discovering the Lost Virtue*. New York: Touchstone, 1999. Book.

Shalit, Wendy. *The Good Girl Revolution—Young Rebels with Self-Esteem and High-Standards*. New York: Ballantine Books, Random House, 2007. Book.

Tannahill, Reay. *Sex in History*. Briar Cliff Manor, NY: Stein and Day, 1980. Book.

Turow, Scott. *Presumed Innocent*. New York: Warner Books, 1987. Book.

Waltke, Bruce K. *Creation and Chaos*. Portland, OR: Western Conservative Baptist Seminary, 1974. Book.

von Rad, Gerhard. *Genesis*. Philadelphia, PA: The Westminster Press, 1973. Book.

Webster's Third International Dictionary. Chicago, IL: G &C Merriam Company, 1971. Dictionary.

Wenham, Gordon J. *Genesis 1-15*. Vol. 1. Word Biblical Commentary. Waco, TX: Word Books, 1987. Commentary.

Note to the Reader

The author invites you to share your response to this book by posting on Truth Encounter or Dave Wyrtzen's Facebook, writing Truth Encounter, PO Box 580, Midlothian, TX 76065 or by email: mail@truthencounter.com.

Please visit www.truthencounter.com and www.25thchapter.com for additional resources and podcast series on related subjects.